# WAYS OF CONFUCIUS
# AND OF CHRIST

# WAYS OF
# CONFUCIUS
## AND OF
# CHRIST

From Prime Minister of China
to Benedictine Monk

by
DOM PIERRE-CÉLESTIN LU, O.S.B.
(LU ZHENGXIANG)

translated by
MICHAEL DERRICK

with an introduction and notes by
JOSHUA R. BROWN

IGNATIUS PRESS    SAN FRANCISCO

Ignatius Press thanks Amanda Clark, Ph.D., and Anthony E. Clark, Ph.D., of Whitworth University, for their invaluable help with the photographs and the permission to use them.

Cover photographs from the Anthony E. Clark Private Collection
Left:
Formal portrait of Lu Zhengxiang in diplomatic regalia during Qing Empire, 1907
Right:
Formal portrait of Dom Pierre-Célestin Lu, O.S.B.
(Lu Zhengxiang)
at Saint Andrew Monastery, Belgium, after his election to titular abbot by Pope Pius XII, 1 August 1946

Cover design by Roxanne Mei Lum

# CONTENTS

# INTRODUCTION

## Joshua R. Brown

A few years ago, I was invited to participate in a panel for a Catholic celebration of the Chinese New Year. As often happens, the question-and-answer period became the best part of the experience, and we panelists found ourselves talking about additional resources of interest for the audience. At one fateful point, another panelist mentioned in passing an internet video clip of a Chinese Catholic monk who had once been prime minister in the Republic of China, named Lu Zhengxiang, also known in English as Dom Pierre-Célestin Lou Tseng-Tsiang.[1] With my own background being primarily in Catholic theology and classical Chinese philosophy, I was unfamiliar with the name, but I had been desperate to find more writings of Chinese Catholic theology. Suffice it to say, I was intrigued and wanted to know more about this Lu fellow. That very afternoon, I placed an order to borrow two Chinese biographies on Lu from my interlibrary loan system.

Reading about Lu's life became an extraordinary experience (particularly in the biography offered by his younger friend, the great Chinese-Taiwanese philosopher,

---

[1] Lou Tseng-Tsiang is equivalent to Lu Zhengxiang; both are romanizations of 陸征祥. "Lou" is rendered following the Wade-Giles system of romanization, which was the dominant system used in Chinese studies for much of the twentieth century. "Lu" is rendered according to the Pinyin system of romanization, which has been dominant in Chinese studies since ca. 2000. See Note on Language Conventions below.

theologian, and churchman Stanislaus Luo Guang).[2] The tremendous obstacles he had faced and the beautiful legacy of faith and charity he had left behind sometimes brought tears to my eyes. Not long after, I searched high and low to find a copy of Lu's *Ways of Confucius and of Christ*, which had gone out of print long ago and was hard to come by. As I read it, I realized that Lu had become, not just an academic interest, but a brother and friend. I was utterly moved by Lu's humility, sincerity (a central Confucian virtue), his finding and losing his beloved wife, Berthe, and the deep love for God and the Church in China that had led him to enter the Benedictines. Eventually, I came to realize that I had incurred a debt of friendship and owed it to Lu to help others come to know him.

Lu's small but powerful book is not an autobiography or memoir per se, but rather a series of recollections he shares about his life. And what a fascinating life it was! Born into an impoverished Protestant household in Shanghai, China, Lu received relatively little formal education and only one year of undergraduate study in French before he took a post as an interpreter for the Chinese diplomatic corps in Saint Petersburg. In 1911, he was received into the Catholic Church and would become one of the most distinguished Chinese Catholics in the history of Chinese public service. Eventually, Lu served as foreign minister and later as prime minister in the nascent Republic of China. In one of the highlights of his distinguished diplomatic career, Lu was heavily involved in representing Chinese interests at the Paris Peace Conference in 1919. After the death of his beloved wife, Berthe, Lu entered Saint Andrew's

---

[2] The two best biographies of Lu I have found are Luo Guang, *Lu Zhengxiang zhuan*, in *Luo Guang quanshu*, vol. 27 (Taipei: Xuesheng shuju, 1996), and Shi Jianguo, *Lu Zhengxiang zhuan* (Shijiazhuang shi: Hebei renmin chubanshe, 1999).

Monastery in Belgium in 1927. Despite having little theological formation and no education in Latin before his novitiate, Lu overcame many difficulties to become a priest in 1935 and a titular abbot in 1946. He died in 1949, sadly, before being able to complete his dream of founding a new Benedictine monastery in China.

If *Ways of Confucius and of Christ* were merely the story of the Chinese diplomat who became a Benedictine monk, that alone would be reason to read it. But as it happens, this book is far more than Lu's story. As we will see below in this introduction, Lu's book was born out of the experience of the German occupation of Belgium during World War II, when he began to tell about his life in order to give hope to his friends and neighbors. Looking at the world around us full of pain and despair, we, too, can be tempted to cast our eyes to Heaven and wonder: "Where have you gone, Lord?" Lu's book is medicine for all troubled souls who question God's love for them and the world, as he recounts how God slowly but surely led Lu to His side, through many vicissitudes, triumphs, and sorrows. For all of us, especially Christians, who need reminders of hope in the divine love that moves the cosmos, Lu's story is a much-needed salve for the soul.

Additionally, Lu's little book is a must-read for any who are interested in Christianity in China. On the one hand, Lu's story is not merely a rehearsal of his life, it is also something of a microcosm of Christianity in China. Like Lu, the Chinese Church has long been subject to the tempestuous winds of Chinese political history and has had to navigate the Chinese suspicion that Christianity was "Western" and, therefore, both un-Chinese and untrustworthy. For Lu, becoming Catholic and eventually a monk and priest did not diminish his Chinese identity, but fulfilled it. Indeed, in the preface to the book, Lu acknowledges the appropriateness of the English title, saying, "For it was indeed Confucianism that guided me toward Christianity, and finally even to the Catholic Church, for the simple reason that the natural order leads directly to the supernatural order and prepares for the reception of the divine graces." Lu understood his Chinese culture, exemplified by Confucianism, to be the fertile ground in which the seeds of faith were sown; his Chinese identity was not discarded in the life of grace, but given new, more abundant life. Hence, Lu's life of patriotic service and faithful love of the Church provide a clear example of how *Chinese* Christianity is genuinely possible (and not just Western Christianity transplanted into China).

In another respect, Lu's story is also a love letter to the Church in China. For Lu, the ultimate end of his life in the monastery and priesthood was not his own happiness, but the spiritual flourishing of his people. Even Lu's decision to enter the Benedictine Order was partly inspired by his master, Xu Jingcheng 許景成. Xu believed that the great treasure of the West was nothing else but the Christian religion, specifically Catholicism, and he advised Lu to study closely and perhaps even enter into the "most ancient society" of this "most ancient branch" of Christianity: "Make yourself its follower, and study the interior life that must be the secret of it. When you have understood and won the secret of that life, when you have grasped the heart and the strength of the religion of Christ, bring them and give them to China." To the end of his life, Lu was inspired by this advice and firmly believed that the Benedictine way of life and spirit could spark the fire of Catholic devotion in China, turning the entire nation to Christ. As both a diplomat and priest, Lu's life was one of continual service to his people. In this respect, Lu's little book gives testimony and inspiration to the enduring hope of many who yearn for the day when the Chinese people en masse will come to know the love and the goodness of the God of Jesus Christ.

We ought to read Lu's story for many reasons, but doing so presents its own challenges. The original edition of *Ways of Confucius and of Christ* was printed in 1948 without an introduction. As we know, much has changed between 1948 and 2023. Therefore, in order to prepare the contemporary reader better to understand and appreciate Lu's story, this present edition offers a few introductory aids: a background to the history of the book and a historical overview of the political situation within which Lu lived and work.

## *Ways of Confucius and of Christ: Background to the Text*

Lu himself says very little about how his book came to be, but his biographers, especially Luo Guang, address this question. In order to understand the genesis of the book, we must begin before 1927, when Lu entered Saint Andrew's Monastery in Bruges, Belgium. Lu's beloved wife, Berthe, was of Belgian nobility, and the couple had moved to Switzerland, to their modest cabin on the shore of Lake Maggiore. Lu had originally purchased the cabin despite a meager salary as a diplomat because of his own frequent needs for convalescence. Lu was well-known for his frail health and constitution—a lingering consequence of malnutrition in infancy because his mother suffered dropsy and had reduced milk supply—and he often needed to retreat to healthier climates for a term in order to manage his duties as a diplomat. However, in 1922, Berthe fell ill with a "cerebral congestion", or apoplexy, and the condition eventually took her life in 1926.

As Berthe's death drew near, Lu considered what to do with his life after Berthe passed. Inspired by the story of Madame Elizabeth Leseur—whose husband had been an atheist and then converted to Catholicism after her death, eventually becoming a Dominican priest—he desired to enter the religious life. Since the couple had been childless, the devout and pious Berthe enthusiastically supported Lu's wish, even as others in the family advised against it. It is worth noting that Lu's entrance into the monastery was inspired by his love for Berthe in the sacrament of marriage. Luo Guang speaks to this love in a beautiful passage worth citing at length:

> What was it that made Lu so resolved to become a monk? For the previous 27 years of his life, he and Berthe had carried out the hardship of the secular life, bearing the troubles and the joys of this world, and knowing the joys of marital love. After Berthe bid her husband a final adieu, her soul went to the joy of the heavenly banquet: an eternal life of singing songs of praise to God, and an eternal life lived in [the] midst of God's love. After her death, Lu also went to a new form of life, one that left behind this world of dust, and locked himself within the monastery. He too would now spend night and day singing songs of praise to God and live in the midst of God's love. Although he could not yet see the face of God or be with Berthe, he knew he shared with her a common form of life, and by this, they were reunited.[3]

Indeed, the link between Lu's marital and monastic lives is one reason why Lu entered Saint Andrew's: it was relatively close to his wife's grave.

At the same time, Lu entered the monastery in order to leave the affairs of the world behind and commit himself

---

[3] Luo, 131–32.

to prayer and the life of devotion to God, in preparation for taking this spiritual gift back to the Chinese people. Upon entering the monastic life, Lu took up a life of predominant silence. It is interesting that Lu's earliest duties as a diplomat had been as a translator in Russia, and at his height, he had argued the cause of China in conferences with other powers. As a monk, his diplomatic voice gave way to the silence of prayer and meditation, no longer hammering out negotiations but communing in friendship with God. To be sure, Lu was still amicable and conversed with his fellow monks warmly, if minimally. His silence was especially evident in his stout refusal of every newspaper journalist who called on him—and there were several—seeking to publish his story to the world. Lu wanted none of the worldly fame or recognition and had no desire to tell his story, even to fellow confreres who asked him. For Lu, that was all in the past, and his life as a monk needed his full attention and presence.

The situation changed, however, in the fateful month of May 1940.[4] In this month, the Nazi army unleashed its stunning *blitzkrieg* on the Netherlands, Belgium, and France, overwhelming each country in turn. Almost immediately, the life of the monks at Saint Andrew's was turned upside down. Luo Guang recounts that during the *blitzkrieg* around 1,500 wounded soldiers became temporary residents of Saint Andrew's and received basic care and spiritual aid from the monks. While Lu had sought to leave the world behind in a holy fashion, the troubles of the world found their way into his new life, and he saw the terrible outcomes of the war firsthand.

Eventually, on March 25, 1942, the German Army commandeered the monastery and evicted the monks of

---

[4] My description of the circumstances of May 1940 and their impact on Lu is based on ibid., 203–5.

Saint Andrew's. Many of the monks, including Lu, were effectively homeless and had to board with friends and relatives in the area around Bruges, while a contingent of the monks went to a sister monastery in Loppem, in order to prepare for the reception of the full community of Saint Andrew's.[5] During this time and after moving to Loppem, Lu experienced the suffering of living in occupied territory: rationed foods, poor diets, and the solemn spreading of gloom. Additionally, Lu's fellow monks were worried about his persistently frail health, as Lu was unable to gain consistent access to fires for warmth or needed medicines. Fortunately, Lu defied the odds and remained in good health, but the suffering around him weighed heavily on his mind. In this context, Lu began to find more spiritual vigor and saw a new mission laid before him.

This mission was to find a way to give the people of Belgium, including his fellow monks, hope and trust in God to see them through their difficult situation. As Luo puts it, Lu wanted to help the people about him see that "God is to them a Great Father, who is concerned not only for their private lives but also for that of their country and their people."[6] In order to communicate this message, Lu turned to what he knew best as a way of communicating God's faithfulness and goodness: his own remarkable life. Luo observes that Lu finally saw a value in telling his story precisely because it was not about him. "He was now thankful to be able to put his story before the eyes of others and did not desire undue glory that might be attributed to his achievements, because he knew himself to be but an ignorant child. Rather, he wanted to give mankind evidence of how God turns with compassion toward the life of a single man."[7]

[5] Interestingly, during this interim period, Lu stayed at the house of Baron Joseph Ryelandt, a famous Belgian Catholic composer of the day.

[6] Luo, 204.

[7] Ibid., 205.

Thus, Lu began writing down his "thoughts and memories" on his amazing life's journey. In one of the very first events where Lu was sharing his story with a small number of friends, German military entered suddenly, took his notes, and disbanded the meeting. In a way, the Nazis were absolutely right to fear what was happening in that salon: Lu's message was indeed a threat to their own mastery in Belgium and an important form of resistance. Thankfully, Lu persevered, and soon many groups began requesting that he share his story with them.

Most likely, when Lu initially gave the lectures that comprise *Ways of Confucius and of Christ*, he had never planned to publish them as a book. The latter came about because of his audience members, many of whom had been touched by the message of grace and hope in his life's story. Luo Guang notes that soon after the Nazis were defeated in 1944, Lu was able to return to Saint Andrew's and resume his life of predominant silence. However, he also received messages from those who had heard his story during the war, who desired to revisit the inspirational message that had given them such hope and comfort, and who found it beneficial to their own lives to reflect on Lu's story. Always a humble servant, Lu picked the four most significant lectures and compiled them into one volume, eventually published as *Ways of Confucius and of Christ.*[8]

### *The Historical Background to Lu's Life*

Lu's message of hope in the God of love still speaks powerfully. However, because Lu's testimony to God's grace is told amidst momentous political events in Chinese history, many who read his story today may be ill-equipped to

---

[8] Ibid., 210.

understand the significance of his message and thus feel it is not for them. This new edition of *Ways of Confucius and of Christ* seeks to help the reader in this respect, primarily through the inclusion of additional notes that explain historical figures and events Lu references. Additionally, given the genuine lack of general knowledge about Chinese history in the English-speaking world, some readers will also benefit from a general background to the period in which Lu's story occurs.

Between his birth in 1871 and his entering the monastic life in 1927, Lu lived and worked during one of the most decisive and chaotic periods of Chinese history. To begin with, Lu was born during the latter stages of the Qing dynasty, which was the last of the imperial dynasties to rule China. The Qing was not technically speaking a Chinese dynasty. Ethnically, what we know as Chinese are the Han people, whereas the Qing rulers were part of a group called the Manchus, which was not a single ethnicity, but a collection of non-Han peoples. The Qing was thus a Manchu dynasty that early on had conceded the need to "sinicize" (that is, make Chinese) some of their practices in governing, while also imposing Manchurian elements on their subjects, such as the wearing of a ponytail, or "queue" (*bianzi* 辫子 in Chinese). Indeed, at the end of the Qing, the refusal to wear a queue became a public sign of resistance to Qing policy and governance (a sign of resistance Lu himself would later adopt).

When the Qing began in 1644, it was ruled by very successful politicians and military leaders. Yet, by the mid-nineteenth century, the world had begun to pass the Qing by in the stream of modernization. As a consequence, late Qing rulers were often completely incapable of fending off outside influence from Western powers (primarily Great Britain, the United States, and France) and Japan. The classic example of this is the growth of the opium trade, which Western merchants transported into China. Opium had a tremendously negative impact on the Chinese social fabric, and the Chinese government sought to curtail the import and sale of the disastrous drug, but lacked the strength for real resistance. Bitter tensions over the opium trade eventually spilled out into actual military conflict between China and Great Britain in the First Opium War. The war was a resounding victory for Great Britain, and they were able to force China to sign the fateful Treaty of Nanjing (often Romanized as Nanking) in 1842.

The Treaty of Nanjing is today recognized as the first of a series of peace pacts between China and Western powers dubbed "the unequal treaties". These were unilateral treaties, meaning they only benefited one party (Western imperial powers), which exacted severe costs from the Qing government. While a total of eighteen countries benefited from the unequal treaties, there were six major beneficiaries: Great Britain, the United States, France, Russia, Germany, and Japan. In these treaties, which China had to sign either due to use of force or under threat of force, the Qing government had to make a series of humiliating concessions to Western powers, including special extraterritoriality rights, forced leases of prime economic land tracts, and special coastal and river navigation rights.[9] Sadly, many missionary privileges such as the right to travel in mainland China were secured through the unequal treaties, which only encouraged the perception of Christians (both Chinese and foreign missionaries) as arms of the opium trade and Western imperialism. As one scholar has observed,

---

[9] Wang Jiangliang, *Unequal Treaties and China*, vol. 1 (Honolulu, Hawaii: Silk Road Press, 2016), 2–10.

"Christian missions ... in the minds of most Chinese, were associated with Western imperialism and opium."[10]

Many of the problems Lu mentions from his diplomatic career were consequences of the era of unequal treaties. For example, one of the most significant clauses won in these treaties was the German control of the Jiaozhou (or Kiaotschou) Bay territory on the Shandong peninsula, which the Germans leased (at a very favorable rate) from China in 1898, in order to gain access to the peninsula's mining resources. When Germany sparked World War I, the Japanese government sided against Germany partially in order to secure Western support for taking over the German lease of the territory. Ultimately, in the Treaty of Versailles—which Lu, in protest, refused to sign—Japan was granted control over German territory in China by the Western powers.

Today, there is little debate that the unequal treaties were exploitative of China and exacted deep costs both in terms of economic losses and in terms of the constant shame and humiliation of the Qing government and the Chinese people. During the nineteenth century, China was a perpetual loser in the eyes of the world: a land with abundant resources led by a weak government and ripe for plunder. Again, the situation at Versailles is illustrative: although China had a seat at the table for international diplomacy, it had no real voice or sway and was unable to defends its own interests.

At the end of the nineteenth century, while Lu was serving as a translator and diplomat in Russia, the situation worsened amid two crises. The first was the war between

---

[10] Jessie G. Lutz, "China and Protestantism: Historical Perspectives, 1807–1949", in *China and Christianity: Burdened Past, Hopeful Future*, ed. Stephen Uhalley Jr. and Xiaoxin Wu (Armonk, N.Y., and London: M.E. Sharpe, 2001), 179–94, 180.

Japan and China, the First Sino-Japanese War of 1894–1895. Begun over a dispute over land on the Korean peninsula, the First Sino-Japanese war was a result of Japanese interests in becoming the dominant superpower in East Asia. Qing generals and the Chinese public were certain China would win the war easily. They were completely mentally unprepared for the defeat China suffered, one that exposed how far China had fallen behind in military strategy and materiel.

This first crisis helped cause the second, the Boxer Uprising of 1899–1900. The Boxers, a term for groups of martial artists in China, began by protesting and attacking Qing government installations. However, they soon turned their ire and violence upon a new target: agents of foreign imperialism, which they believed (correctly in some degree) had weakened China and exploited her. The most opportune target for the Boxers happened to be Christians. During the uprising, hundreds of foreign missionaries and thousands of Chinese Christians lost their lives, with many later declared martyrs of the Church. The Qing government at the time, led by the infamous Empress Dowager Cixi, gave tacit acceptance to the Boxers and refused to intervene. Ultimately an alliance of Western powers led by Great Britain, France, and the United States invaded, eventually gaining control of Beijing and bringing the uprising to an end.

Afterward, the Western powers forced China to sign the Boxer Protocol of 1901, which exacted tremendous economic reparations from China. Consequently, the Boxer Protocol was yet another and perhaps the greatest source of deep shame and humiliation for China. Yet even for patriotic servants like Lu, the Boxer Protocol was complex. Although the terms were devastating, the genuine failures of the Qing court in the uprising were apparent. Additionally, Lu had a personal stake when his beloved master, Xu Jingcheng, was scapegoated, executed, and then posthumously exonerated six months later by the failing regime. By the end of the nineteenth century, then, the question was not so much if but when the Qing would finally fall. After some last-ditch efforts at reform, the last Qing ruler finally abdicated in 1912.

During the middle of Lu's diplomatic career, China underwent a profound transformation from an imperial monarchy to a republic. The transition was by no means smooth, as Lu testifies. Part of the problem was tension in the government. The first president of republican China was Yuan Shikai, a former Qing general. Yuan's role had been negotiated as part of the terms of the Qing emperor's abdication, and he was not truly committed to the idea of the republic (evidenced by the fact that Yuan attempted to resurrect the imperial system in 1915 by proclaiming himself emperor). The real heart and soul of Chinese republicanism was Dr. Sun Yat-sen, a medical doctor and Methodist Christian (though scholars debate his devotion to Christianity) who admired American democracy. While Yuan headed the government, most of the elected repre-sentatives and officials were members of Sun's Guomin-dang (Kuomintang or KMT) alliance, and the two sides did not abide well. A famous example was the assassination of KMT leader Song Jiaoren in 1913, long suspected to have been arranged by Yuan and his associates.

Notably, it was during this period that Lu became a politician serving as head of the foreign ministry and then as prime minister. Lu's own account is that, as a nonpar-tisan, he was unable to make any positive movement as prime minister and resigned after two months, citing his frail health. At any rate, it is certain that although Lu was a full supporter of Chinese republicanism and held great affection for Sun Yat-sen, he became quickly disenchanted with Chinese politics and sought to leave public life altogether in 1921. It was only the economic need to care for his wife, Berthe, that forced him back into the diplomatic ranks in 1922. Undoubtedly, two significant events contributed to Lu's disenchantment. One was mentioned briefly above. In 1919, Lu represented Chinese interests at the Paris Peace Conference, only to find that the Western powers still saw China as a pie to be carved up and, in this case, handed to Japan. This disappointment, however, is actually dependent upon an earlier event that led to Lu's disenchantment. In 1915, during the early stages of the First World War, Japan sent China a list of demands now known as the Twenty-One Demands. The Twenty-One Demands were quite breathtaking in scope.[11] Primarily, their terms focused on confirming Japanese power over Shandong and Manchuria, but also included humiliating terms of cultural impositions. For example, the Japanese government demanded the "right to preach" in China, meaning the right to distribute pro-Japanese propaganda freely throughout China. Lu was appointed by Yuan to be the initial negotiator of the demands, and Lu was steadfast in refusing many of them. Ultimately, however, Yuan worked around Lu to negotiate with Japan himself and succeeded only in refusing the most humiliating of the cultural impositions of the demands.

For these reasons among many others, Lu left public life, though he retained contacts and friendships with Chinese diplomats even after he entered Saint Andrew's in 1927. Between 1927 and 1948, when Lu's book was published in

[11] For an excellent discussion of the Twenty-One Demands, including Lu's place in the drama, see Niroko Kawamura, *Turbulence in the Pacific: Japanese-U.S. Relations during World War I* (Westport, Conn.: Praeger, 2000), 11–24.

English, there are two historical events we must mention. The first occurred in 1937, when Japan launched a brutal invasion of the Chinese mainland (known in China as the Second Sino-Japanese War, but also seen as the beginning of World War II). The Japanese invasion produced stories much like the Nazi campaigns did in the West, such as the "Rape of Nanjing (Nanking)", in which Japan slaughtered hundreds of thousands of Chinese people, including large numbers of civilians. For Lu, the experience of the European context of World War II was also impacted by the often-devastating news from China, and his heart was moved by both tragedies.

At the time, China was governed by the KMT coalition government, led by Generalissimo Chiang Kai-shek. Chiang was himself a devout Christian—it was he and his wife who commissioned the Catholic writer and lawyer John C. H. Wu to translate the Psalms and the New Testament into classical Chinese.[12] Yet although Chiang was a deeply sympathetic figure for many like Lu, the war with Japan left the KMT terribly exhausted. Unfortunately, attempts at holding China together failed, and China descended into a bloody civil war between the KMT and the Chinese Communist Party (CCP), led by Mao Zedong. As we know today, the CCP finally emerged victorious, and Chiang Kai-shek officially resigned from his office on January 21, 1949, just six days after Lu's death.

Truly, Lu Zhengxiang was a man doomed to live in interesting times. Yet it is fitting to note that January 15, 1949, marked the twenty-year anniversary of Lu's perpetual vows as a Benedictine. Despite the shifting sands of his professional career, the tragic loss of his wife, and the

---

[12] This story is related in John C. H. Wu, *Beyond East and West* (Notre Dame, Ind.: Notre Dame Press, 2018), 288–91.

long-sufferings of his beloved country, Lu had found a path to know the quiet, still goodness of God in his life as a monk. Although Lu had many dreams as a monk that were left unfulfilled and incomplete when he passed, he realized his greatest dream. For Lu had gone into the ancient school of spiritual cultivation to imitate the joy of his wife in Heaven and know God in a deeper and truer way. In the end, he passed in this happiness of knowing God's love in a full and intimate way. And now, the Church today can be thankful that this often silent monk was moved by God to share his story with us, so that now his story can help us also come to know the same peace and friendship with the Lord that sustained the awe-inspiring and beautiful life of Lu Zhengxiang.

## Note on Language Conventions

The original edition of *Ways of Confucius and of Christ* utilized a version of the Wade-Giles system for Romanizing Mandarin Chinese. Since the year 2000, Pinyin has been adopted as the standard in both Chinese-speaking communities and in the Western academy. For readers who would like to engage in further reading on the people, places, and themes mentioned in Lu's narrative, any further research will usually depend upon Pinyin renderings. Thus, for this edition of *Ways of Confucius and of Christ*, I have updated the Romanization to Pinyin when Lu's references are clear, including updating from Peking to Beijing and Nanking to Nanjing, even though the older Romanizations remain in some use today. The only exceptions are the names of Chinese figures, such as Sun Yat-sen and Chiang Kai-shek, which are almost exclusively known in the West under the older Romanization style. It is also likely helpful to note for readers unfamiliar with Chinese names that in Chinese convention, the surname comes first. Our author is from the Lu clan, and Zhengxiang is his primary given name, hence he is called Fr. Lu or Dom Lu (Dom being a French title of respect for Benedictine monks).

Additionally, Lu's original book was published in French. In the English translation published as *Ways of Confucius and of Christ*, the British publisher and translator retained the use of French titles and abbreviations, such as "M." for "Monsieur" and "Père" for "Father" in reference to priests, in addition to including untranslated French and Latin phrases. For this edition, I have erred on the side of adopting conventions more familiar to the contemporary English reader ("Mr." instead of "M." and "Madame" instead of the abbreviation "Mme.") and have rendered translations of non-English phrases, often in parentheses so as to conserve the French or Latin for readers familiar with those languages.

# AUTHOR'S PREFACE TO
# THE ORIGINAL EDITION

THESE pages do not constitute my memoirs. They do no more than bring together some memories and reflections. They were written in Belgium, during the German occupation, in the course of the year 1943, at the request of my brethren, the monks of the Abbey of Saint Andrew, near Bruges, who had on several occasions expressed to me the desire to know in more detail the principal events of my public career and, indeed, the story of my life. Not to delay longer in responding to that token of brotherly sympathy, I made a selection from my more outstanding memories and set them forth in the form of discourses.

In writing these discourses, my thoughts have continually been turned toward my friends of bygone days, to whom my withdrawal and my entry into the religious life had not failed to cause some astonishment. I like to believe that these writings may enable them to understand the progress of my life more easily. They will find therein the witness to my fidelity to my country and to my deep affection for them all. This book being, moreover, published for their sake, the very simple form that I have wished to give it will provide, I hope, a witness to my sincerity for the generality of my readers.

If Providence should lead me one day to write my memoirs, I could only do so in my maternal Chinese language, which alone can express the thoughts in my mind and the feelings in my heart in all their meaning.

The original edition of this book appeared in the French language at Bruges, in the month of March 1945, under the title *Souvenirs et Pensées*. Translations in nine different languages were in preparation within a year.

I gladly agreed to a suggestion made to me that the English edition should appear under a title directing attention to the providential ways I have been led to follow: *Ways of Confucius and of Christ*. For it was indeed Confucianism that guided me toward Christianity, and finally even to the Catholic Church, for the simple reason that the natural order leads directly to the supernatural order and prepares for the reception of the divine graces.

In a time so troubled as our own, it may be useful for more than one man who hesitates in the appreciation of spiritual values to address himself fully to the natural order and to perceive the truth and the strength and the vitality that are in it. This experience, and the honesty with which he draws his conclusions from it and seeks to press them home to the end, may lead him by roads of which readers of this book will discover the plan.

Some English friends, having read the French edition, have expressed the desire to see me take that itinerary farther. To meet their kind request, I am addressing a message to them: a "Letter to My Friends in Great Britain and America". May it not too greatly disappoint their expectations.

The recent war gave me the opportunity to know for myself what it is to live under an occupation imposed on a free country by a totalitarian enemy power whose secret state police meddle in every affair of public and private life. I had to take account of it. It was as well for me. On July 25, 1942, as I was giving a discourse on religion in Bruges, in the *salon* of the Baron Ryelandt, the meeting was interrupted by the sudden entry of three agents of the Gestapo.

They forbade me to speak, and, seizing my manuscript, they carried it off. After a certain delay, they ordered the audience to disperse, detaining everybody present elsewhere in order to take note of their identity.

I believe I respond to the expectation of my readers in adding to one of these discourses a short passage to express my thought on this Second World War and, more especially, on the responsibility of the statesmen who found themselves incapable of foreseeing and preventing it.

On the day on which I left the world to assume the habit of the monks of Saint Benedict, October 4, 1927, I believed it to be my duty to acquaint the king of the Belgians of the step I was taking in embracing the religious life in a monastery of his country.

I had been, in 1914, a special ambassador in his country, and in that circumstance, as again later in 1919, King Albert had condescended to show me a gracious goodwill and a confidence of which I respectfully retain the lively recollection.

In the letter I addressed to the sovereign, I sought to pay homage to him for the spiritual wealth for which I am indebted to my life's companion, who was a subject of the king of the Belgians and who, by her Christian manners, discreet and delicate, had greatly contributed, unknown to herself, in preparing a religious vocation in me.

Animated by a profound respect for the venerated memory of that unforgettable head of the state, for Her Majesty Queen Elisabeth, and for their august son, His Majesty Léopold III, whose incomparable moral greatness and high political perception will one day be appreciated by the whole world, I do myself the great honor of reproducing, at the end of this preface, a reproduction of the autograph letter that His Majesty Albert, King of the Belgians, condescended to address to me on October 16, 1927. It gives these *Ways of Confucius and of Christ* a preface whose value could not be exceeded.

I should like this little book to be a modest testimony of gratitude to the goodness of God on behalf of my poor person and to the justice of His Providence on behalf of my dear country.

I dedicate it to the blessed memory of those to whom, after God, I owe most happiness on this earth: to my respected parents, Mr. Lu Yunfeng and Madame Lu, *née* Wu Jinling; to the glorious memory of my master, the Minister Xu Jingcheng; and to the much-loved memory of my wife, Berthe Lu Zhengxiang, *née* Bovy.

In their persons, and in all things, may God be glorified.

### Letter from Albert I, King of the Belgians

Brussels October 16, 1927

To the excellent and reverend Father Lu,

It is with great feeling that I read the touching homage that you offered in memory of the dearly missed Madame Lu, my compatriot, in the letter you wrote to me on the occasion of your entrance into the illustrious Order of Saint Benedict.

I very much appreciate the confidence that you have shown in relating to me the sentiments that contributed to your holy vocation.

The memory of the diplomatic mission that you fulfilled with my government in 1914 remains with me as well as your sympathy for Belgium's loss.

To consecrate oneself entirely to the service of Our Lord alone can confer, upon those who consent to be touched with this grace, the peace of the soul that is the highest happiness in this life.

In commending myself to your prayers, my Reverend Father, I assure you of my most profound esteem.

Albert

# MY VOCATION IN DIPLOMACY

## (1871–1906)

*February 1943*

A FTER fifteen years of the monastic life and seven in the priesthood, passed in an almost complete seclusion, how is it that Providence now seems, when I am seventy-one years old, to lead me to speech and to action?

Often, in their sympathy, my friends have been surprised that I should maintain an almost total silence. On more than one occasion, they have wanted to question me, asking me what is the road that I have traveled, from private life into public, and even to the control of the foreign policy of my country—such was my career as a diplomatist and as minister for foreign affairs—and how from public life God led me to the monastic life and to the priestly state, and how, it may be, He leads me now to the apostolate.

I am about to try to trace for you the outlines of my life. It is summarized in a very few words. I have striven all my life, to the best of my ability, so to behave as to see clearly and to walk straightly, not to let myself knowingly be blinded by any prejudices or any fear, and perpetually to reconsider my deeds and my duties in the light of experience, of reflection, and of our common dependence upon Heaven.

What has my life been worth? Heaven will judge it. But you would please me if, at the end of my story, you would join with me in praying to God that my poor qualities may bear witness to His goodness and to His majesty.

I was born in Shanghai. My father, Lu Yunfeng, belonged to a well-to-do family. He had married, in 1854, Mademoiselle Wu Jinling. She brought into the world a little girl who lived only a few weeks. By the will of God, my parents then knew trials and poverty and the great mortification of remaining childless for seventeen years. I was born on June 12, 1871, a puny baby. My mother, in giving birth to me, contracted a dropsy that eight years later was to carry her off. Her premature death is a source of grief to me to this day. I accepted and I accept that burden; to lighten it, I join in the joy of those who still have their mother or who kept her for longer than I.

How can I express my gratitude to my father and my mother? My father was a religious man, honest and clearsighted. He loved me with a complete unselfishness and was quite beyond the reach of the bitter representations that my entry, at the age of thirteen, into the School of Modern Languages at Shanghai[1] brought him from every quarter. The pupils of this school were regarded as traitors in the making, who, with the aid of these languages, would deliver their country to foreigners.[2] From my childhood, my parents taught me to face critics among men and the vicissitudes of life; and my father taught me also never to become fond of money. "Money", he said, "should fall between the hands like water off a duck's back; a man cannot retain for himself what is a medium of exchange for the good of all."

---

[1] The school in Chinese is called *Guang Fangyan guan* 廣方言館.—Ed.

[2] Schools like the one Lu entered were staffed by Westerners, often missionaries, contributing to the suspicious view of them by traditional-minded Chinese.—Ed.

My father was a Protestant catechist. He used to go out every morning distributing tracts, and especially Bibles. I have inherited from him the habit of circulating useful literature, and it has never seemed to me that money spent in this way is money wasted. We belonged to the London Missionary Society. It was in this Protestant society that in 1873 I received baptism at the hands of the pastor, Dr. William Muirhead, and that I met Christian charity for the first time, being still a child. I could give a thousand touching instances of it. Protestantism has been for me a stage without which I think I should not have been able to reach Catholicism. I have the deepest gratitude for all the charity and kindness shown toward me by these missionaries. There is necessarily a rivalry between Catholic and Protestant missionaries. When it exists in a dignified atmosphere, it edifies souls and brings them together. When it becomes competition, it excites the passions, sets truth aside, and diminishes morally those who would congratulate themselves on doing down their neighbor. It was, therefore, with real delight that when I entered the monastery I read in the Rule of Saint Benedict, in the chapter on "The Instruments of Good Works", the fine principle: *honorare omnes homines* (honor all people).

After some private instruction in the Chinese classics, therefore, at the age of thirteen and a half, I was entered in the School of Foreign Languages at Shanghai.[3] There I specialized in French. This course was given by a zealous master, Mr. Alphonse Bottu. When I was eighteen, my studies were interrupted for a whole year by a grave illness, the very same that had carried off my poor mother. Nobody thought I would recover from it. God saved my

---

[3] This is the same school mentioned previously, the *Guang Fangyan guan*. —Ed.

life. I managed to make up the time lost in my studies, and at twenty-one I left for Beijing, being admitted to Tong Wen College, a school for interpreters attached to the Department for Foreign Affairs.

At Beijing I continued the study of the French language and literature, under the direction of Mr. Charles Vapereau, a distinguished professor with whom I was afterward to continue in association until his death. I was not envisaging a diplomatic career, to which admission was open only to students who had completed their Chinese classical studies, but I was anxious to spend a fairly considerable period abroad, so as to hold on my return a position in the postal administration. I was, therefore, in no way looking for a political career, and my father, who perceived all the corruption to which the officials of the imperial dynasty abandoned themselves, wanted nothing in the world less than that I should include myself among them.

My assiduity in study meant that I spent only one year in the Tong Wen College.

By a providential coincidence of circumstances, I was sent, in December 1892, to be a fourth-class interpreter at the Chinese legation at Saint Petersburg. I was going to find there a master who, by his lessons and by his example, caused me to pass from private into public life, for which, without having ever thought of doing so, my father had himself given me the best of preparations.

In the thought and the practice of Confucianism, filial piety and the work of personal perfection are the real education of statesmen. The mission of the statesman is to ensure the public welfare. To obtain that, one thing in particular matters: "to develop the natural virtues in the hearts of all men".[4] That social development of the natural virtues is,

---

[4] *Da Xue* (The greater learning), 1.

for the statesman, a primordial task. It can only be taught in the bosom of the family, the family being the ultimate unit of society. What higher role than that of the father of a family, who, in the modest surroundings of his home, is called upon to bring up his sons for so lofty a vocation!

Confucianist doctrine is essentially the traditional wisdom of the ancient kings, wise men and virtuous, whose high characters open the national history of China—in the third millenary before Christ, Yao, Shun, and Yu; in the second millenary, Tang, King Wen, and King Wu. The documents of this wisdom were compiled, collected, and published by Confucius in the sixth century before Christ. He made verbal commentaries on them, and his commentaries and his lessons, collected and developed by his immediate disciples, represent an immortal statement of first principles. These works together constitute our thirteen classics. China has lived, and still lives today, by this philosophy and this education.[5] She owes to them the line and the endurance of her strong family traditions, thanks to which our people have remained serene, and even happy, in the midst of trials and have not ceased to increase and develop. She also owes to them the poise of her political spirit and of her traditions of government, which are based directly on the principle of family life. In a word, we have not, through the course of our history, given our favor to the formulation of seductive theories but, from generation to generation, following the example and according to the precepts of our ancestors, we have applied ourselves to fathoming the laws that govern human nature and to conforming ourselves with earnestness to them, ceaselessly studying the fruits of our experience and observation.

[5] The imperial examination system based upon Confucian education was abolished in 1905. The basic formation in Confucian education, however, remained important in China for many years after. The formation was suppressed, however, in the infamous Cultural Revolution of 1966–1976.—Ed.

In order that a young man may learn to develop the qualities of his intelligence, of his judgment, and of his heart, and thereby to school himself for social, civic, and political life, it is, then, in the first place necessary that he should honor his parents. For that he must obey them and love them; he must not dispute what they say, but must strive to understand them and to enter into their thought. If it should be really necessary, he must learn how to enlighten them and how to ensure the greatest good for them. In the society of his brothers and sisters, the child is initiated into the behavior that must be his in the society of men. He must not be selfish; he must love his brothers; he must not rate himself in his own mind above them; he must not envy them; he must not draw attention to their faults or their shortcomings but must tactfully make good the deficiencies of others. It is according to this practical system, strengthened by experience, that a young Chinese must strive, within his family, to learn how to govern himself and to prepare himself for the government of a family, for the government of a city, of a province, or even of the state, for whichever Heaven may have given him the necessary capacity, and for whichever he may be able to receive the vocation from Heaven.

This family training is essentially balanced. It avoids the excesses of prejudice and precipitancy; it prefers the study of reality and the observation of nature and, in particular, of the nature of man to intellectual trifling; it is founded on the authority of the head of the family, and it goes back right to the principle of all authority, which is God, the Creator, that Providence which humbles the proud and raises up the meek; it seeks the acquisition of wisdom, and, as a first step in that direction, it prescribes above all the fulfillment of the duties of one's condition; one has to do, here and now, what one ought to do, and, in doing it, one has to clarify one's sight, so as to practice seeing farther and farther ahead; one has to avoid every unworthy ambition and to concentrate on being useful to others. One has not to be vainglorious in the high positions one may be able to attain, but to keep on the road to the acquisition of wisdom. "The man who discovers wisdom in the morning may die in the evening."[6] What regard for moral distinction and for intellectual stature! What awareness of the dignity of the human soul and, may one say, of its immortality!

These ideas are the very essence of Chinese civilization and family life. One finds them, in varying degrees, in all those ancient families that are so numerous in our country, as much in the towns as in the countryside. Those families form closed societies, where the stranger seldom gains access. Alas, if one judges a country without knowing its best families, one is completely unaware of its character.

Children are told of the example of the three great emperors, Yao, Shun, and Yu, the contemporaries of Abraham, Isaac, and Jacob. The classical Chinese books tell in particular that "Shun was indeed a sovereign." "He had abandoned the empire without more regrets than if he was discarding an old pair of shoes." "He was great in dignity! He was master of the empire, and he always remained indifferent to his own greatness!"[7] There is the spirit, the atmosphere, and the context in which our most ancient national traditions conceive of training for public life. There are the standards according to which a young Chinese can and must learn to serve the community and the state, and the standard according to which an old Chinese who loves the young judges them, with an interior burning desire to find among them this constant moving,

---

[6] *Analects of Confucius*, 4.8.
[7] *Mencius*, bks. 3A:4 and 7A:35.

this daily striving toward wisdom—that search for wisdom which suggests many points of resemblance between the school of Confucius and that of Saint Benedict. It is further said of both that, still eminently youthful, they overcome their age by their maturity.

And that is why, be it said in passing, the Benedictine spirit practiced in China—because it is a matter of practice and not of words—could not fail to draw countless sons into the Church and to fill the monasteries with legions of monks ...

However ill I may have observed these precepts, the poor attempt at following them that I have made has guided me constantly in life. I have put into practice to the best of my ability the testament of my father, which is expressed in a single word: *Tian*—trust in Heaven.[8]

We are, then, in January 1893. I was then twenty-one and a half years old, and I arrived at our legation in Saint Petersburg, there to fulfill the functions of an interpreter. I was to spend fourteen years there, from 1893 to 1906, under the successive direction of three chiefs: Mr. Xu Jingcheng, from 1893 to 1897, Mr. Yan You, from 1897 to 1903, and Mr. Hu Weitai, from 1903 to 1906.[9] During this same period, the Russian Department for Foreign Affairs was in the charge of four ministers: Mr. Ghiers, who

---

[8] When Lu left for St. Petersburg, his father gave him a tablet bearing the word *Tian* 天. Often translated as "Heaven", *Tian* has many meanings in classical Chinese, including that of a reference to the high God of the Zhou dynasty (which included the time of Confucius' life). The term was also used by Catholic missionaries as part of the preferred term for God, *Tianzhu* 天主 or "Lord of Heaven". While "trust" is not part of the meaning of *Tian*, the addition of extended meanings to important characters is an acceptable practice in literary Chinese.—Ed.

[9] These latter men are better known as Yang Ru 樣儒 and Hu Weide 胡維德.
—Ed.

was a sick man and who died shortly after my arrival in Saint Petersburg; and then, successively, Prince Lobanov, Count Mouraviev, and Count Lamsdorf, with whom my duties as an interpreter, and very often as *chargé d'affaires*, brought me into regular and frequent personal contact. I had through them a chance of initiating myself into the duties of a foreign minister, which were in the future to fall to me. I was able to begin this initiation, and my whole diplomatic education, under the direction of the eminent master whom Providence had prescribed for me, in the person of my first chief, Mr. Xu Jingcheng. That statesman, upright and clearsighted, honored me with his confidence and his devotion, almost every day spending long hours in preparing me for the task that he envisaged for me. Without him, I would never have become a diplomatist, and, ultimately, I would not have become either a monk or a priest.

Mr. Xu Jingcheng had caused me to come from Beijing. When he learned of my intention to confine myself to a few years abroad, he addressed a remonstration to me: "You deceive me. How, being entered in a school founded for the Department for Foreign Affairs, can you think of utilizing for a private career the education you have there received? Why do you act thus?" "I want to console my father's old age." "Then write to your father. If he is able to dispense with you, and to entrust you to the training I intend to give you, I am going to try to make a diplomatist of you."

At once I understood the severity of the duties that the public service imposes. I offered myself to accept them. With his lofty unselfishness, my father approved my decision. Alas, I was about to live abroad for eleven unbroken years and was not again to see that well-beloved father to whom I am profoundly devoted for all that I owe to him and for the moral grandeur with which he gave so elevated a love to his son. [10]

Periods of decadence have a singular attraction for those who live in them. To embark upon their reform, it is necessary to some extent to be ignorant of their manners. In China, I had known neither the world of officialdom nor society. Mr. Xu gave me as a first rule that of not attaching myself to the declining régime; neither to enter into it nor to condemn it, but to confine myself to doing my duty and, while studying the most distinguished servants of the European countries, to make a program of life and action for myself. And for that, to learn to hold my tongue, whatever might be the humiliations and the insults inevitably inflicted on me by, on the one hand, Chinese dignitaries despising everyone who did not flatter them, and, on the other, European officials and European society calling the whole Chinese state "the sick man" and considering every Chinese an inferior being.

The problem is worth the trouble of considering it a little more closely. I had attended a function at the Winter Palace in Saint Petersburg. The emperor and the empress had received 3,000 guests and had themselves opened the ball. At this same time, the rules of the Imperial Chinese Court required that officials of the first rank received by the emperor should present themselves prostrate on the ground before him, and, further, in the field of international relations, when the emperor of China received the credentials of a foreign envoy, the audience took place in the Hall of the Vassals. Contemplating this contrast, Mr.

[10] The care of aged parents is a traditionally important form of filial piety in Confucian culture. To his credit, Lu requested leave to see his father twice before Lu Yunfeng passed, but both requests were rejected.—Ed.

Xu said to me: "Watch, keep silent, and, when the hour comes, reform."[11]

It was in this atmosphere of silence, of revolution, and of action that all my public life was spent. I never lingered over abuses I had not the power to stop or over their consequences, even catastrophic, that were to lead to the fall of the dynasty and were to lead China to within a hair's breadth of her ruin. Who would have been able to stem so violent a murky current? God Himself refuses to save man when man refuses salvation. And Mr. Xu continued: "When these men fall, take care that you are ready, not to cast stones at them, but immediately to replace them, so as to begin in China a modern work of construction, according to a plan both ancient and new, for the realization of which you will not have wasted an instant in preparing yourself."

To carry out such a program, it is necessary to learn to love everybody and to act alone. That is not a life of solitude; it is a life of isolation.

My master prescribed that I should Europeanize myself for love of China. How would I have been able to follow these instructions if my countrymen had succeeded in keeping me in ignorance of foreign countries or if foreign countries had led me to disparage my own country? In every period of transition, the two opposing currents are very violent. To escape from them, one must be prepared to be judged unfavorably by both. So one must learn to be alone. The Christian life, for its part, does not escape this rule. Our Lord Jesus Christ is so often all alone on His Cross.

Mr. Xu desired for China a complete rejuvenation, and he desired that in every sphere the country should emerge

[11] Xu's meaning is that China ought to learn means of foreign diplomacy from Western nations.—Ed.

from the condition of stagnation in which the best ancestral traditions, deformed and become sterile, were leading to a result diametrically opposed to the spirit that had given them birth and that had enabled them in the past to give us our finest epochs of richness and splendor. He wanted a modernization that should cause the spirit of Yao, of Shun, and of Yu to live again in the world of today. He studied Europe, seeking to grasp the principle of its best institutions, the source of its progress, seeking to discover, in order to win them and to give them to China, the moral forces that assured the balance of European society and to distinguish them sharply from the forces, from the passions and infatuations, that compromised that balance.

Christianity, the Church, and in particular the Catholic Church imposed themselves on the respectful attention of Mr. Xu. He had been struck by the existence of a worldwide spiritual government, of which the history went back right to the Founder of the Christian religion. So as to study this fact more closely, in the course of a journey that took him to Europe, he had stopped in Rome and had there spent the Christmas holidays. I remember very clearly the first conversation in which he spoke to me of it, giving to the expression of his thought, as he often liked to do, the form of a fable. He had got me to call at his home, and he began thus:

"One day the minister of commerce in England noticed the arrival and the entry into the country of a new commodity, previously unknown in Europe—tea; ten chests of tea, coming from China. The following year the number of these cases increased tenfold. Two years later it rose to a thousand.

"Surprised by the unexpected growth of this import, he called a tree-planter and bade him set out for China and there study the cultivation of tea, instructing him to choose some of its finest seeds and then to betake himself to Ceylon, in order there to introduce this crop, so that England might no longer need to purchase her tea in China."

Mr. Xu went on: "The strength of Europe is not to be found in her armaments; it is not to be found in her science; it is to be found in her religion. In the course of your diplomatic career, you will have occasion to study the Christian religion. It comprehends various branches and societies. Take the most ancient branch of that religion, that which goes back most nearly to its origins. Enter into it. Study its doctrine, practice its commandments, observe its government, closely follow all its works. And later on, when you have ended your career, perhaps you will have the opportunity to go still farther. In this most ancient branch, choose the most ancient society. If you can do so, enter into it also. Make yourself its follower, and study the interior life that must be the secret of it. When you have understood and won the secret of that life, when you have grasped the heart and the strength of the religion of Christ, bring them and give them to China."[12]

I hear him still. He continued: "You are from Shanghai. Have you seen the foundation at Zikawei?" I had to confess that I did not know it. The foundation at Zikawei, as you will hardly be unaware, was a gift of the Minister of State Paul Xu[13] converted to the Catholic Faith by the

---

[12] Some have portrayed Xu Jingcheng as a Catholic, but I have found no evidence to support this. There is, however, even today in China the phenomenon of "cultural Christians", consisting of nonpractitioners of Christianity who nonetheless revere and study the tradition—it seems fair to categorize Xu as such a cultural Christian.—Ed.

[13] In the local pronunciation of Shanghai, the family name of Xu is pronounced "Zi", whence the name of Zikawei. ["Zikawei" is the Shanghai dialect for *Xujiahui* or "Xu family plot" and is home to the famous St. Ignatius Cathedral and other important Shanghai Catholic institutions, including schools and universities, over its long history.—Ed.]

Jesuit Father Matteo Ricci, in that seventeenth century which might have marked the beginning of the evangelization and the modernization of China. You know also, alas, how the long quarrel over the rites, by its spate of inept and sterile passions and arguments, destroyed the magnificent work undertaken with such vision by the missionaries of those days, the intellectual and moral work that would have endowed the Catholic apostolate with a strength and with a vitality from which one would have been able to expect the complete regeneration of our society and our country.

Mr. Xu said to me: "Study, then, what was done three centuries ago at Zikawei. And see what has come of it." In those few words he set before me the whole problem of the relations between China and Christianity, the whole of that missionary question which had to wait for the pontificates of Benedict XV, of Pius XI, and of His Holiness Pius XII before its solution could be begun.[14]

If Mr. Xu were alive today, he would be profoundly happy; he would see China, victorious over herself, treated by the powers on a footing of equality; in his clarity of vision, he would rejoice to see the Church, freed of her former shackles, coming into contact with our country in a new fashion, on the solid foundation of a direct understanding with the Chinese state, in an atmosphere of mutual respect and sympathy, of understanding, of independence, and of cooperation.

I ought to tell you something of my professional activity as a young diplomatist at Saint Petersburg. I accompanied the

---

[14] In the light of p. 116 below, Lu seems to be referring here to the Chinese Rites Controversy, in which aspects of Chinese cultural participation were forbidden for Catholics from 1704–1939. Under Pius XII, the Vatican promulgated *Plane compertum* in 1939, relaxing the restrictions from previous centuries. —Ed.

minister on all his calls, and I had to translate successively, with speed and precision, from Chinese into French and from French into Chinese, all his conversations with the Russian minister for foreign affairs and with his colleagues of the Diplomatic Corps. I was the only member of our legation to fulfill this function, and whenever the minister was absent, I saw myself invested with the functions of *chargé d'affaires*, virtually holding in my own hands the relations between the Chinese government and the Russian government. This was a difficult school, very valuable to anyone in a position to understand its importance and to draw forth its lessons.

I should need many pages to sketch the history of those fourteen years of diplomatic life. It was set in the saddest and most humiliating period of the general history of my country. One of the decisive steps, which led to our fall, was taken in Saint Petersburg.

I had been six months in the Russian capital when my chief took me for the first time to the house of the minister for foreign affairs. Presented to Prince Lobanov as an interpreter, I seemed so young that he could not prevent himself from remarking, "You bring me, then, a little boy..." I was not put out of countenance, either at this time or later. So three years afterward, at the time of the visit of the viceroy of Tianjin, the famous Li Hongzhang,[15] leader of our delegation to the coronation of Nicholas II, the prince, with whom I had already been in the relation of a *chargé d'affaires*, took it into his head to praise me to the viceroy. These words from the mouth of a minister for

[15] Though Li Hongzhang's official position was overseeing Zhili province in Northern China, he became the effective diplomatic voice of China in negotiations with Western powers for many years.—Ed.

foreign affairs, whose political designs I had been resist-
ing, were, at this beginning of my career, a windfall that
might be called providential. Li Hongzhang replied in the
same terms, saying that if the Chinese government had
appointed me, it was because it knew me so well.

It was during this visit to Saint Petersburg that Li Hongzhang concluded with Russia a secret defensive treaty,
which attracted the attention of every chancellery and
of which I only learned the text when I read it at the
Ministry for Foreign Affairs in Beijing, on the day when
I became the head of that department. In return for this
alliance, China had authorized Russia to build the Trans-
Manchurian Railway, known as the Chinese Railway of
the East, and had granted the Russians full rights in it for
eighty years. In the end, the treaty brought us no military
assistance, giving great benefits to Russia without any cor-
responding benefits to us.

The term of office of Count Mouraviev was a melancholy one for China. The minister advocated a policy of
violence. Our defeat in the war with Japan in 1894 had
revealed the extent of our feebleness to the whole world,
and Count Mouraviev intended not to delay in profiting
from it and compelling us to lease Port Arthur and Dalny
to Russia for twenty-five years. That was the last drop that
made the cup overflow.[16] Germany demanded Jiaozhou,
England claimed Weihaiwei,[17] France took Guangzhou-
wan.[18] And then the Boxer Uprising broke out in China.
Its suppression by the combined powers inaugurated the
hardest period of our humiliations. The Beijing Protocol
of 1900 will remain one of the most cruel, wicked, and

---

[16] This occurred in 1898.—Ed.
[17] An important naval port in Shandong province.—Ed.
[18] A territory in Zhanjiang province.—Ed.

blind acts of the whole of the world's diplomatic history.[19] In the exactions that it imposed upon us, which were spread over a period of forty years, it perhaps exceeded in injustice any other treaty to which an independent people has ever had to surrender itself.[20]

At the time when Russia was indicating these demands to us, Mr. Xu had left Saint Petersburg for Berlin. The government recalled him to Saint Petersburg, with the title of special envoy, charging him to carry out the negotiations in collaboration with his successor, Mr. Yan You. I was the interpreter at all the conferences between Count Mouraviev and our two ministers. Finally, it was necessary to yield.

Count Mouraviev, in his Chinese policy, went against the opinion of the emperor, who, under the influence of Prince Oucktomsky, inclined to more moderation. When the storm had broken in China, the emperor made lively representations to Count Mouraviev. Next day, Mouraviev, by whom up to that moment I had been received every morning, was found dead in his room at the Department for Foreign Affairs. This whole affair proved to be a catastrophe both from the public and from the private points of view. Count Lamsdorf succeeded Count Mouraviev.

During the Boxer Uprising, Manchuria[21] had been occupied by Russian troops. Mr. Yan You entered into negotiations for the liberation and the return of that part of

[19] This is a reference to what is more commonly known as the Boxer Protocol, which was accepted in December of 1900 and ended the Boxer Uprising. Notably, Li Hongzhang helped negotiate the treaty.—Ed.

[20] Lu is referring here to Article VI of the Boxer Protocol published in 1901, indemnifying China for a debt of "450,000,000 Haikwan taels", to be paid to the Eight Powers (with interest) over a period of thirty-nine years (one year had passed between acceptance of the treaty and its official publication).—Ed.

[21] An area of Northeast China, bordering Russia.—Ed.

our national soil. The negotiations broke down, and again, God knows with what dramatic consequences . . .

Mr. Yan You died in office. His successor, Mr. Hu Weitai, was a former school and college friend of mine.

While he was in charge of our legation, suddenly, on February 8, 1904, Japan, without a declaration of war, attacked the Russian fleet outside Port Arthur. I happened to be actually in Beijing, spending six months' leave in China after eleven years of uninterrupted residence abroad. Providence ordained that in returning to Saint Petersburg I should take the ship that was returning the Russian diplomatic personnel to Europe. The Russo-Japanese War was about to deprive Russia of Port Arthur and Dalny, which she had wrested from us seven years before, and, in addition, to despoil Russia of the chief fruits of her activity in the Far East.[22]

What can a young man think whose life begins in the midst of so redoubtable a series of international conflicts, invariably settled by threats and violence, and in which is carried on an impassioned struggle of national and personal prides, which the least exacerbation pushes to despair and to vengeance, and all for the perpetual humiliation of the weak, to whom is never spared either insolence or insults?

What could I do, then, if not strengthen myself interiorly in meditating upon the great thoughts that Chinese philosophy offers for the instruction of those young men who dare to enter into life as it is?

My principal thoughts were centered around a saying of Mencius, our great philosopher of the fourth century

---

[22] Russia lost the Russo-Japanese war of 1904–1905 and, under the terms of the Treaty of Portsmouth, was forced to cede many important Russian holdings in China to Japan.—Ed.

before Christ, to which my master Xu had not ceased to call my attention:

> When Heaven wishes to impose a great mission upon a man, it deems it proper at first to fill his heart with bitterness, to subject his nerves and his bones to weariness, to deliver his whole body to the torments of hunger, to reduce him and to exhaust him, frustrating and overthrowing all his undertakings. In this manner it gives strength to his heart, endows his will with endurance; it increases him in stature and gives him the power to carry out that of which he would have been incapable.[23]

To the young Christians who will read these lines I permit myself to say: if it should be given to you at times to know a certain temptation of discouragement, raise up your hearts on high, and, reflecting on what these non-Christian philosophers wrote twenty-four centuries ago, see then whether you have not very much more reason than they to regard life with that victorious serenity which, let it be said between ourselves, has only one foundation: in faith and in humility.

But for all that, God never abandons those who trust in Him. While the tragic events were taking place that gave me so much reason for apprehension, both professionally, as a diplomatist, and as a patriot, the Lord waited for the occasion to relieve my isolation by giving me, in the midst of so much conflict and so much misery, a providential and powerful support, whose warm encouragement was more precious to me than I can convey by words. He was to give me at the same time, and of this I will speak to you later, a lesson in heroism before which a true heart has no longer the power of holding itself back.

[23] *Mencius*, bk. 6B:15.

It was during my residence in Saint Petersburg that I met Mademoiselle Berthe Bovy, granddaughter and daughter of Belgian officers—her grandfather was a general, her father a major—and a relation of the Belgian minister at Saint Petersburg. I loved the distinction of her thought and of her spiritual life, her sound judgment, her disinterestedness, her courage, and her loyalty. We were joined in marriage on February 12, 1899, in the Catholic parish church of Saint Catherine, in the presence of the parish priest, the Dominican Father Lagrange.

Our spirits and our hearts were made for one another. I found in Madame Lu a veritable life's companion, exceedingly dear, a collaborator who instantly seized upon the heart of a matter and, without ever being distracted by secondary considerations, carried out her duty with simplicity. You know how, being a Protestant, I promised to bring up in the Catholic religion the children whom God might give us. In the following years, I did not understand why Providence deprived us of the joy of having children. I had to wait a very long time before seeing that that sacrifice was the necessary condition of the religious and priestly vocation for which, from that time onward, God was preparing me.

My chiefs were opposed to my marriage to a foreigner. We took no notice of their dissatisfaction, and my wife had the courage and the unselfishness to accept that incomprehension which for eight years excluded her from all the receptions to which I was invited. That trial came to an end of its own accord on the day when I became minister at The Hague. But then, surrounded with honors, she maintained a similar aloofness in all circumstances, never wishing to take advantage of her husband's position to give herself airs with anyone, least of all with the compatriots of her country of origin or her country of adoption. When

King Albert died, I was honored with a very kind letter from Her Royal Highness the Duchess of Vendôme, telling me how much her late brother had appreciated this very rare discretion in my wife, who, during the twenty-seven years of our marriage, gave all its beauty to our life together and brought into my heart an overwhelming love and gratitude. Her equanimity of mind and the delicacy of her sensibility made it truly said, "Dans le salon de Madame Lu, on ne dit pas de mal du prochain"—no one speaks ill of his neighbor in Madame Lu's drawing room. There was in her a true Christian wisdom and, as a good Chinese, I add, a true Confucianist wisdom.

I have sketched for you the principles of the Confucianist education that Mr. Xu had sought to give me. Those principles governed my chief's relations with our government, whose attention he never ceased to draw to the decadence of our institutions and to the designs among foreign powers to which that decadence led. The imperial Chinese government was offended by his suggestions and by his persistence and refused to consider what he said. In order to get rid of his importunity, responsibility was attributed to Mr. Xu for the diplomatic defeats which the Imperial Court and government were irremediably bringing down upon our country. When the Boxer Uprising broke out, they sought to make him a scapegoat for the internal disorders and the reprisals from abroad that his advice, if it had been taken, would have made it possible to avoid. By an imperial edict, Mr. Xu was condemned to be beheaded in the marketplace at Beijing, and this edict was carried out within twenty-four hours, on the morning of July 29, 1900.

That act of iniquity was committed when I was exactly halfway through my fourteen years' residence at Saint

Petersburg, and while Mr. Yan You was in charge of our legation. I must add that the decree of decapitation was followed six months afterward by a second decree, futile enough, of rehabilitation.

So the problem of my vocation in public life or of my return to private life was set before me in all its sharpness. My master, to whom I owe all my training, was the innocent victim of the incompetence of the great, of their pride and of their jealousy. What would be the good, I said to myself, of serving a governing class so unjust, so blind, and so cunning? For a whole year I had to wrestle with myself to remain in the public service for which this master, now beheaded, had sought to prepare me.

Mr. Yan You could not fail to notice the struggle that was going on within me. So he did me the great service of pointing out my duty to me: "You will avenge your master in remaining worthy of him and in carrying out the program for which he has sacrificed his life." With the help of God, I understood that any hesitation in the face of that duty would be a desertion. Public life in the service of justice and of the state was definitely the one and only field in which I would consecrate and concentrate the exercise of my feeble strength for the integral accomplishment of my duty as a man.

# MY POLITICAL CAREER

## (1906–1920)

*March 1943*

MY residence in Saint Petersburg continued until 1906. In the year before that I had been appointed counsellor of the legation. I spent little time in that position; one year later, the government appointed me a minister plenipotentiary and charged me with the opening of a legation at The Hague, where until that time our affairs had been looked after by our minister to Berlin. Emperor Nicholas II, informed of my departure, condescended to express the desire to receive me. This was something quite without precedent. In the course of the audience, at Tsarkoié-Sélo, an audience that was extremely cordial, the emperor expressed to me the hope of seeing me again at Saint Petersburg as Chinese minister, and he conferred on me the *Grand Cordon* of Saint Stanislas. And at this audience I had the surprise and the great honor of seeing the empress come in, allow me to offer her my homage, and condescend to address to me a most gracious *au revoir*.

At this period of my public life, there took place an incident, apparently slight, which was very characteristic of this time in the history of the modernization of China.

The reigning imperial dynasty, of Manchu origin, had since its accession to the throne in 1644 obliged all

Chinese to wear a *queue*, and that under pain of death. At the beginning of the twentieth century, the leaders of the revolution spontaneously refused to carry any longer the humiliating badge of a closed era. I was counsellor at Saint Petersburg. I waited no longer. Without having consulted the minister, in agreement, however, with certain other members of the legation, we cut off our *queues*. Mr. Hu Weitai, a little astonished, heartily sharing in our opinion, did nothing; but when I was promoted to be head of our legation at The Hague, he drew my attention to the gravity of an act that would be described as a schoolboy's gesture and that would not fail to be judged with severity by the imperial government. He suggested that I should wear a false *queue*, for soon after my arrival at The Hague I would have to receive in that city a high commission of enquiry, presided over by the viceroy of Nanjing and by the minister of public instruction, and come to the West to study at first hand the working of the constitutional laws of the European states. This commission, he observed, would not fail to make a report against me at Beijing.

I could not bring myself to commit for the sake of my personal security an act that appeared to me like a retreat, at a time when the country had so much need of being made to advance, and it appeared to me that the time had at last come for a highly placed official to join the movement for emancipation that was spreading among the *literati* within the country and among the students abroad. I had the opportunity of being presented to the high commissioners before their arrival at The Hague at a banquet that the Chinese students in Paris were giving in their honor. The circumstances in which I met them for the first time did not permit them to mark their astonishment in any excessive manner. The viceroy of Nanjing contented himself

with a smile, the minister of public instruction with a
frown. There the incident remained.

Two years later, returning to China, instead of going
immediately to Beijing, I stopped at Tianjin and from
there informed the minister for foreign affairs that I would
have to remain six months in that city before I should be
able to present myself in the capital, since I had cut off my
*queue* and that time was necessary for it to grow again. The
minister replied that he authorized me to present myself
freely at the department without wearing a *queue*, but that
he asked me, for the only visits that I would have to make,
to the prince regent and to the prime minister, Prince
Qing, to wear a false one. The question of principle being
conceded, I did not insist any more, and for those two
visits I submitted myself voluntarily to what was not more
than a formality.

At the moment when I assumed personal responsibility
for a legation of China, the memory of my master, Xu,
to whom I owed my education and who had died as the
victim of his duty, came back to my mind and to my heart
more insistently than ever. I was very profoundly aware
of the gratitude I owed him and that our country owes
him. I wanted to translate this feeling into a deed and to
relieve my conscience of a duty. I decided to set aside the
sum paid to me as my first month's salary to have a medal
struck, showing his sadly missed features. I was able to
offer this medal in silver to Her Majesty the Queen of the
Netherlands, to the emperor of Austria-Hungary, to the
emperor of Russia, and to a great number of high officials in China. After that, up to the time when I took my
solemn vows as a Benedictine monk, in 1932, it was an
intimate joy and comfort to me, whenever an opportunity
presented itself, to offer a copy of this medal to personal

friends who might be able to understand its importance and significance.

I remained four years at The Hague.

A very short time after my arrival, I presented to the minister for foreign affairs, Mr. van Tets van Goudriaan, a proposal for an agreement for the establishment of Chinese consulates in the Netherlands Indies, a colony in which China has a large number of citizens. This proposal for a consular agreement, several times put forward by the Chinese government, had always met with a systematic opposition on the part of the Netherlands Colonial Department. From my first overtures, Mr. van Tets refused absolutely to adopt a new point of view.

While these discussions were going on, The Hague became the scene of the meeting of the Second International Peace Conference, which met in that city in the course of the summer of 1907. The Chinese government appointed me as its ambassador to this conference. That task brought me for the first time face to face with the simultaneous attitude of all the powers, unanimous in treating China as a country of the lowest rank. This was an experience very rich in lessons for me.

At the conclusion of the conference, I set out for Egypt, intending there to spend some weeks of leave, and, rather than be promoted to a more important post, as I could expect to be, I asked my government to reappoint me as minister to The Hague, so that I might again address myself to and pursue the negotiations for the consular agreement, to which my countrymen in the Netherlands Indies justly attached the greatest value. Meanwhile, my friend Mr. van Swinderen, whom I had known well in Saint Petersburg, had succeeded Mr. van Tets as Netherlands minister for foreign affairs, and I was confident of finding in him a breadth of view advantageous to our two countries.

Nevertheless, the negotiations dragged on. The Netherlands minister for the colonies persisted obstinately in his opposition. I judged that in the circumstances it was profitless for us to maintain a minister at The Hague permanently, and I suggested confidentially to my government that I might be recalled to Beijing. My recall dismayed Mr. van Swinderen. Understanding that it was no longer possible to insist on refusing a decision that was imposing itself, he made energetic representations to his colleague of the Colonies, and with such good effect that the negotiations followed me to Beijing, where I continued them with Mr. Beelaerts van Blokland, Netherlands minister to my government. They proceeded, not without difficulties, to a satisfactory conclusion. The establishment of the consulates was gained.

In 1911, I returned to The Hague for the exchange of the instruments of ratification, and from there I went on to Saint Petersburg, whither I was sent by my government as a special commissioner for the revision of the Treaty of Commerce by Land Transport concluded in 1881 between China and Russia. In Saint Petersburg, following the recall to Beijing of Mr. Sa Yindou, I was then appointed minister of China. The kind wish of Emperor Nicholas II was realized, and I came back to Saint Petersburg to resume there many dear friendships that my fourteen years' stay had permitted me to form and to receive from the emperor, from the Russian government, and in particular from Mr. Sazonov, the minister for foreign affairs, the most cordial welcome.

We were planning, my wife and I, a whole series of receptions in the rooms of our legation reserved for entertaining, which we had refurnished with taste, when the abrupt development of political events in China obliged us to countermand the arrangements already made.

Passing through its final phase, which was to be victorious, the Chinese National Revolution was gaining ground every day and was threatening the imperial dynasty. It gave a political role of the first importance to our legation at Saint Petersburg. The change of régime was near. It was going to put a very rapid end to my stay in the Russian capital; of this I had no doubt at all.

But before tracing the outline of these great political events, I must speak to you of the interior evolution of a religious character that was going forward in me and that, as my public career unfolded itself, had led me to the decision to abandon Protestantism and to seek admission into the Catholic Church.

I had been married ten years, and God had given us no children.

The disposition in which I had promised to bring up our children in the Catholic religion arose out of a feeling of respect for the most ancient form of Christian worship and for the dignity with which my wife carried out her Christian duties. Without entering upon a profound discussion of the object of the religious controversies of which Europe has been the scene, still less of the controversies themselves (and this attitude is shared by many of my countrymen); recognizing the apostolic origins of the Roman Church, and confining myself to agreeing that heresies and dissidences have the effect of bringing a greater precision and clarity in the matters disputed, it seemed to me that the time had come for me to take a step forward; to draw closer to Jesus Christ, the living Source of our religion, and to seek admission into the communion of the Holy Catholic and Roman Church, professing my belief in what she teaches and undertaking to practice what she prescribes. I found in the Catholic Church unity of government, unity of doctrine, and unity of precept; I saw in her a sure guide for the conscience and a stable foundation for society and for the state.

My wife had never raised the question of religion with me. She had confined herself to carrying out the obligations of her conscience with much simplicity. This discretion itself led me still more to desire to join the Catholic Church, which I would not have allowed myself to consider entering if she had sought to push me toward it.

It was in Beijing, during the period there that followed my recall from The Hague, that I disclosed to her my intention of becoming a Catholic. She was delighted. I had just been appointed special commissioner in Saint Petersburg. We agreed that I should await our arrival in that city to ask Father Lagrange, the parish priest of Saint Catherine's, who had married us twelve years before, to receive my profession of faith.

In the rush of visiting that falls to a newly appointed minister, the priest at Saint Catherine's was very much surprised to see me arriving at his house right when I began to take over the post. It was October 25, 1911. I acquainted him with the object of my call. He received it with great delight. Without more ado, he set me a series of questions on the principal points of faith in Christian doctrine. Then he added: "You do not know how to make your profession of faith. Reply in all simplicity to the questions I am going to put to you. After that, I shall take you into my chapel, and, inasmuch as there may be some doubt about the validity of your former baptism, I shall baptize you conditionally."

When I was back at the legation, with what joy did I seek out and embrace my wife, who was not at all expecting this—that without any longer formalities than these I should that very day have joined the Catholic religion. The last division that could have existed between her and me had disappeared. Shortly afterward, I made my First Communion, and on April 5, 1912, I was confirmed by His Grace, the Catholic archbishop of Saint Petersburg.

Meanwhile, as I have just been telling you, the Chinese Revolution was galloping through its last stages and was on the point of triumphing.

Our classical books have a balanced doctrine on the foundation of the principle of authority in public affairs, which represents a just expression of the Natural Law. The supreme power is a mandate from Heaven.[1] That mandate is delicate. If the mandatory does not carry out his duty, Heaven withdraws its mandate from him, and does it through the voice of the people. This is the historic role of public opinion in all countries where men are capable of thought.

For several decades, the Imperial Court had plainly been left behind by events, and its entourage of idle and flattering officials put it in no position to be aware of the progress of events, of the vices of the administration, or of the profoundly unhappy condition of the entire nation that so much abuse of power and so many failings of power kept in a deplorably low state. Military and diplomatic defeats had been piling up, and the dynasty, instead of listening to the clearsighted citizens who were suggesting reforms to it, implacably pursued all those whom it knew or suspected to be imbued with the new spirit.

This time the movement of national revolution and renovation was prevailing throughout the entire nation,

---

[1] This refers to the classical Chinese doctrine, especially affiliated with Confucianism, on *Tianming* 天命, the "Mandate of Heaven" that especially was thought to govern the rise and fall of dynastic rulers, usually by elevating the worthy to rule and casting down those who fall into moral decline.—Ed.

and foreign capitals were following it with the most vigilant attention.

You know who was the leader of this movement.

For twenty-five years, Dr. Sun Yat-sen, a physician from Canton, a Protestant by religion, had been touring China and the world in order to associate together, within the country and abroad, all those of our countrymen who shared his convictions and his desire for action. He sought to persuade the entire nation *to renew itself*, to put an end to the series of iniquitous encroachments that the Powers had permitted themselves in our country since 1840 and that Chinese good sense, in a judgment not lacking in irony, had dubbed "the unequal treaties".

The imperial Chinese government had set a price on the head of Dr. Sun, and a celebrated incident of which our legation in London had been the scene had led me, in accordance with the instructions of Mr. Xu, to follow closely from 1896 onward all the moves of Dr. Sun Yat-sen in the campaign of national rehabilitation that he had undertaken.

The leader of our renaissance had given profound study to the social and political life of the West; its foundations, its merits, its deficiencies, and its errors. He had taken his stand by the principles of the Constitution of the United States, taking up for us the famous conclusion of Lincoln's speech at Gettysburg: "that the Nation shall, under God, have a new birth of freedom, and that the Government of the People, by the People, and for the People shall not perish from the earth."

Dr. Sun Yat-sen was keenly concerned about social questions, intelligent, and impartial. He was clearsighted, and he had sacrificed his life a hundred times. What is still more remarkable, this innovator, this revolutionary who had had to confine himself through several decades to the role of a theorist, possessed an exceedingly balanced intelligence, to such an extent that in all his work, which covers the ethnological and social, the political and economic fields, there is not a principle, not a line that could not be entirely harmonized with the requirements of Catholic teaching.

Since 1896 I had been following this movement with the most lively attention. After the death of my master, Xu, in 1900, I gave my whole heart to it. Since the dynasty refused to save itself, it became necessary to ensure that the country should not be dragged down with it in its collapse; a collapse that from day to day had been becoming inevitable, so that by this time it was imminent.

On December 31, 1911, against the wishes of the entire staff of the legation at Saint Petersburg, and contrary to the advice of all the heads of our missions to Europe, which my devoted and faithful friend Mr. Wang Chonghui, then secretary to our legation, had suggested that I should respectively inform and consult, I took it upon myself to telegraph to the emperor that the dynasty had no foreign support and that, to avoid bloodshed, the blood of our princes themselves, the hour had come for the sovereign to renounce the throne. The emperor hesitated endlessly. Finally, on February 12, 1912, he abdicated in favor of the republic and charged a high imperial official, Mr. Yuan Shikai, to draw up the new form of the state.

Already at Nanjing, Dr. Sun Yat-sen had been proclaimed president of the republic. With an abnegation that accorded well with his moral stature, he retired in favor of Mr. Yuan Shikai. At the same time the provisional Parliament, by a practically unanimous vote, invited me to return to the country in order there to take over the direction of our foreign policy.

How wonderful was that return to Beijing, after twenty years of residence abroad, with the task of reconstructing the Department for Foreign Affairs and of giving a new tone and a new spirit to our relations with all foreign countries! The capital was in a ferment, political circles were seething, and the whole country was disturbed and agitated.

The work of national renovation, possible at last, called for immense labor, immense both in depth and in extent, for which a legion of public men of a proved competence would have been required, whom the nation, left to itself, had not had the means of producing and training.

The corps of civil servants was afflicted with all the miseries that a persistent favoritism had provoked and developed in a veritable time of "decline and fall". On the other hand, the majority of the reformers were newcomers in politics. The political genius of the founder of the republic, his disinterestedness and that of a great number of his supporters, could not give them the experience and professional training that the career of a statesman demands. There were also, necessarily, among the masses of those who applauded the renovation, a battalion of place-hunters, who wanted to profit from this historical moment to grasp the controls and to continue for their own benefit the abuses of the late régime.

By good fortune, the men forming the government found in the person of the president of the republic, Mr. Yuan Shikai, a statesman of great ability who dominated the complex situation of our country and saw clearly the end to be attained and the roads that led there. He was a guide and a powerful support for his colleagues. It took him less than two years to bring order into the principal departments of the internal administration. The nation, recognizing his worth, expected from him a movement in the direction of progress, and the whole diplomatic corps saw in him the ordained restorer of the Chinese state.

By ill fortune, all this future was compromised, and our country came in danger of being irremediably lost, through the personal ambition of Mr. Yuan Shikai, who three years later was to restore for his own profit an imperial power of which the nation wanted no more.

Abroad, our revolution had received a first movement of sympathy, which was soon followed by a new incomprehension and a long period of derision. All that we were doing, all that we were thinking, was *a priori* discredited and ridiculed. The Powers asked each other with a keen interest whether the hour had not come for them to profit by our difficulties and to increase their political and economic encroachments into our country and to begin definitively a collective domination of the whole territory of China. Our two neighbors, Russia and Japan, were the most eager of them all.

The Department for Foreign Affairs had the thankless task of defending a country that was passing through a great national crisis and that had neither any military forces nor any civil administration worthy of the name with which to back up the readjustment of the unilateral treaties that had followed one another in a formidable series and with which also, and above all, to prevent this period of encroachments and interference from dragging on indefinitely.

China, as Dr. Sun Yat-sen had a hundred times declared, had become the colonial field of all the Powers with which she maintained relations, and the foreign understanding that we were to be exploited made of our country what Dr. Sun called "not a colony but a *hypercolony*". How could the position be better described than by adding that the diplomatic corps in China, in which I always counted very good personal friends, formed a partnership in which the members made common cause whenever the interest of one or another among them was in question? The minister for foreign affairs, already harassed, became then besieged, having to face a combination of fourteen partners united against him.

I resolved, so far as might be possible, to keep myself completely outside domestic politics, leaving to my colleagues a task for which my long residence abroad had deprived me of all competence.

It so came about that, despite the changes in the government, which were numerous during the first years of the republic, my prolonged presence at the Department for Foreign Affairs, and especially my return each time the international situation became tense, permitted me to realize my dearest wish, the political testament of Mr. Xu Jingcheng; that is to say, the reform of the Department for Foreign Affairs and the establishment of a professionalized diplomatic corps, in preparation for the readjustment of the unequal treaties.

For that reform I took my inspiration from the Belgian and French models, and before returning to China in 1912, I had made a point of passing through Brussels and Paris in order to examine and to study on the spot the working of the Departments for Foreign Affairs of Belgium and France.

So far as professional diplomacy was concerned, I laid down three new principles that governed recruiting: first, the introduction of examinations in diplomatic practice and the rigorous exclusion of the system of recommendation and favoritism customary until that time; secondly, interprovincial recruiting, making it possible for candidates from all over the country to meet each other in a common collaboration in the service of the state; and thirdly, the selection of candidates who had studied abroad the different languages necessary for the progress of the department.

This new personnel, little by little, came to fill the various sections of the department and was sent to our legations and consulates abroad. At the end of a dozen years, these young diplomatists held most of the senior positions. They opened the way, and their retention to this day in a good number of capitals is a testimony to their competence and to the real service that they have rendered and do not cease to render to our country.

This reform, however, did not change the foreign attitude toward us as quickly as we had hoped and did not soothe the often troubled atmosphere in which we had to carry out our difficult mission.

The first cabinet of the republic, presided over by Mr. Dang Zhaoyi, had an ephemeral existence. The head of the state insisted that I should form the second cabinet, the Chamber having rejected all the names that had been proposed to it. Despite my reluctance to enter into domestic politics, I accepted the office of prime minister provisionally, resolved to continue to devote the best of my activity to our relations with foreign countries and to the establishment of a professional diplomacy. The task was sufficient to absorb the energies of a stronger man than I.

At that moment, Mr. Sazonov, Russian minister for foreign affairs, wishing to profit by our good personal relations, demanded from China the settlement of the question of Outer Mongolia, of which, in the guise of independence, he wanted to make a Russian sphere of influence, whereas that province is an integral part of our country. Chinese parliamentary opinion began to bestir itself, without taking into account that the general condition of our country hardly permitted us to stand up to the foreigner from one day to the next, still less to put an end to his importunities. We were obliged to make a bargain.

Parliament rejected the provisions of the treaty to which I had been able to lead Mr. Sazonov. This refusal involved my dismissal and irritated the Russians, who soon demanded more. Then Parliament understood that it was necessary to yield, and it voted for a treaty much less favorable than the first. The territorial integrity of the Chinese state was happily saved, but nobody was under any illusion about the meaning of its words, and we were going to have to endure new violations of our rights and new painful humiliations for a very long time yet.

The epoch that had opened was, then, very far from a series of successes.

In the course of these difficult years, during which I fulfilled the duties of minister for foreign affairs without any considerable break, China encountered two severe ordeals and one profound disillusionment. The first of the ordeals, an external one, came to us from Japan; the second was caused by the head of the Chinese state himself and opened a period of fifteen years of internal disturbances and civil wars. The disillusionment was imposed on us by the Great Powers meeting at Versailles.

Thanks be to God, none of these blows finally overcame us.

In January 1915, Japan addressed to us an ultimatum of "Twenty-One Demands", of which she demanded the immediate acceptance. The figure of twenty-one in itself shows the truly enormous character of the concessions that Japan sought to arrogate to herself. The European war had been in progress for six months, and our neighbor, on the look-out for every opportunity, profited by that conflagration to make a private attack on us without any of the Powers having the chance of intervening or interposing.

Germany, as I have remarked already, had in 1897 seized from us the bay of Jiaozhou. Japan, in the name of the Allies, had just taken it from the Germans, in order, she declared, to restore it to China. And here was Japan, by an ultimatum of "Twenty-One Demands", demanding from China recognition as the successor of Germany on Chinese soil. She went on from there to draw up a whole program of pretensions to exclusive rights and privileges in the province of Shandong, in Manchuria and Mongolia, in the valley of the Blue River, all along the coast of China, and in the province of Fujian. What is more, we were required to hand over to our neighbor the right of "advising" our government—that is to say, of directing it—and the right of providing police wherever in China she might think fit. Finally, under the plea of "preaching rights", we should have had to authorize Japan to develop a spiritual, moral, and certainly political Japanese propaganda all over the country. Which means that we should have had to surrender to her all that we were and all that we possessed: minds, bodies, and goods.

Chinese public opinion reacted with an extreme vehemence. The country wanted a refusal, pure and simple, to be our only reply to such outrageous demands. But it was reluctant to take into account that such a refusal would have given Japan exactly the opportunity she sought for overthrowing us completely with a single blow and imposing on us a domination that our lack of civil and military organization would not have permitted us to throw off for many decades, if not for many centuries.

I was not in charge of foreign affairs at the time when this ultimatum was handed to us. The head of the state appealed to me, and, however well I knew what a thankless task I was undertaking, I believed it my duty to sacrifice myself and to accept the direction of negotiations infallibly destined for a failure that might bring upon me the incomprehension and dissatisfaction of a large number of my countrymen.

When the negotiations opened, the Japanese minister in Beijing, Mr. Hioki, formally acquainted me with his desire that our conferences should begin in the morning and continue until the evening. This ambitious timetable was the first point in our discussions, and it in itself shows the attitude our adversaries had adopted. Nevertheless, they had to climb down about it.

The conferences, which were limited to the afternoon hours, were prolonged somewhat longer than Mr. Hioki had reckoned for.

By dint of persistence and patience we succeeded at the end of three months in setting aside the six most formidable demands that Japan had congratulated herself on extorting from us, under the ceaselessly reiterated threat of that military intervention that corresponded to her most evident desires and that, at that time, would certainly have been a very easy triumphal progress across our whole country. Among the demands we were able thus to set aside, I recall particularly the pretension to impose Japanese political and military advisers on our central government, to place the Chinese police under Japanese control, and to obtain the right of preaching in China, which would have led to an unbridled Japanese propaganda being freely developed throughout the country and among all classes. Force obliged us to resign ourselves to accepting provisionally the other demands concerning Jiaozhou Bay and the exclusive privileges I have cited above.

All China was indignant, protested, accused.... The time had not yet come when military resistance was possible for us, and this lamentable inferiority obliged us to endure a profound humiliation.

Alas, at this very moment a new crisis awaited us, an internal crisis, which was to increase the disturbance of the country considerably, to delay her restoration, and everywhere to raise up a great many oppositions and divisions, of which none could foresee either the consequences or the end. In breach of his constitutional oath, Mr. Yuan Shikai was working for the reestablishment of the empire for his personal advantage and the advantage of his eldest son and his children.

I then experienced one of the saddest periods of my public life. I had wished to confine myself to foreign affairs; I had seen in Mr. Yuan Shikai the only man who was at that time capable of leading the state; and that man was advancing toward his ruin, while I remained powerless to turn him away, in however small a degree, from his fatal design.

Very cleverly he furthered among those around him his plans for an imperial restoration. I attempted a compromise and proposed that he should maintain the republic and take the presidency of it for life. My suggestion pleased the country, and it seemed to please the president. But other influences soon got the upper hand. He published the proclamation of a new Imperial Cycle.

What was to become of China? How would the initial progress that I had seen accomplished under the guidance of Mr. Yuan Shikai be maintained, and how would it be continued? After long and melancholy consideration, I resolved to follow the president so far as I was able, and I accepted, in addition to the functions of minister for foreign affairs, those of secretary of state in the new régime installed by him. In my conscience, I had clearly decided my line of conduct. Ready to assume all tasks compatible with duty, I was resolved inflexibly to refuse all personal advantages one might have sought to gain from it.

One day the head of the state communicated to me a series of decrees by which in the first place I was myself created a marquis, and thereafter all the more important members of the government were ennobled.[2] To the sharp annoyance of Mr. Yuan Shikai, I refused for myself the honors that were offered me.

That was one of my last audiences with him.

A short time afterward, the president was compelled to withdraw the Imperial Cycle that he had proclaimed, and some weeks later the frustration of his attempt led to his death.

The moral blow that he had sustained had been too much for him. All his protégés, on whom he had showered his favors, had abandoned him, and the marshals of the old régime, whose personal ambitions he had encouraged and on whom he had believed himself able to rely, were suddenly to find the ground clear for plunging China into a civil war that became chronic, ruining the country, oppressing the people, putting a stop to all chance of reform and of progress, and leading China, which sought to modernize herself, to be the laughingstock of the world.

We had to wait until 1928 before the country found again, under a great and disinterested leader, reasonably republican, the unity and the order of which the benefit was quickly to lead to all the great steps that our nation needed so much to take and to carry through to a happy conclusion.

Meanwhile, the European war was raging and stretching the web of its alliances and coalitions across the entire globe.

---

[2] The honorific title "Marquis" (typically the translation for *hou* 侯) was a title used in enfeoffment in imperial China and, thus, a nod to returning (in some manner) to the former style of governance.—Ed.

Since the outbreak of the conflagration, I had been among the small number of those who believed that it would fall to China to take part in it and wanted to see our country take her stand among the Allies. We wanted to settle our account for the initial seizure by which, in 1897, Germany had taken Jiaozhou Bay from us, and we wanted to prevent that violation of our national soil from being followed by the same thing on the part of an Allied country, to its advantage and at our expense. China ranged herself among the Allies.

But when she asserted her just rights, she came up against a secret agreement by which France, Britain, and Italy, in consideration of the help of Japan in this First World War, had promised Japan that they would not support the Chinese claims.

It was as minister for foreign affairs that I assumed the position of leader of our delegation to the Peace Conference. In vain did we make every effort to prevent the Peace Treaty from sanctioning so unjust an agreement to the detriment of an allied country and to avoid the prolongation and extension by the Powers, instead of the healing, of the profoundly troubled conditions that had then for nearly eighty years compromised the relations of China with the West and, for a quarter of a century, her relations with Japan.[3]

---

[3] Here, Lu is referring to the final agreement of the Treaty of Versailles. Article 128 of the treaty stipulated that Germany would cede back to China all rights won in the Boxer Protocol of 1901. At the same time, Article 130 emphasized that the agreement with the other powers remained in full force. Most egregious in Lu's eyes were undoubtedly Articles 156–58, which transferred the rights to the German-controlled Shandong and Jiaozhou Bay areas to Japan. These territories were economically important and, thus, valuable resources handed over to Japan by the Allied Powers. The text of Article 156 explicitly states that all rights Germany won in the 1898 treaty with China, which included the exploitative lease of Jiaozhou and Shandong, were to be

I had appointed my eminent collaborator and dear friend Mr. Wellington Koo to be our spokesman before the Council of Ten, to which had been attributed the power of settling everything.

The situation in the Far East was dominated by the ultimatum of the Twenty-One Demands. When Mr. Koo presented himself before this Council of Ten, he was astounded to hear Mr. Lloyd George put a question to him: "The Twenty-One Demands—what's that?"[4] That openly proclaimed ignorance was not accompanied by any desire for information. The cause of China was judged before it was heard.

Nevertheless, despite this moral blockade, we began about this time to see some sincere friendships growing up around us, in particular on the part of certain American statesmen. The United States delegation to the Peace Conference showed toward us many signs of understanding and many acts of kindness. The United States were in the following years to follow a policy of friendship toward us that was very precious to us.

How could I fail to tell now of the attitude that King Albert of the Belgians took toward us?

It was in the course of an audience at the Palais de Bruxelles, some weeks after the conclusion of the Versailles Conference, in the month of September 1919. I was accompanied by my dear and devoted friend Mr. Wei Zhunzou, former Chinese minister in Brussels The king

completely transferred to Japan, completely bypassing Chinese claims over their own territory. It is worth noting that Japan is listed among the principal powers of the treaty alongside the U.S., France, Great Britain, and Italy, and Japan had representatives on the Council of Ten. —Ed.

[4] A reference to David Lloyd George, prime minister of the UK from 1916 to 1922 and a major framer of the Treaty of Versailles.—Ed.

questioned me with a frankness and a sympathy that struck me very much. I soon saw that he was permitting me to recount to him in plain language the whole drama of the relations of China with the West. The audience went on for more than an hour. The sovereign begged me to indicate to him the sources to which he could refer to find out more about the subject. He offered immediate aid to China. That was not possible. But I asked him to let China count on his support and his devotion on the day when the revision of the unequal treaties between China and the Powers should begin. He agreed wholeheartedly and gave his word.

On the death of the sovereign, Mr. Vandervelde, a former minister for foreign affairs, published an autograph letter that the king had addressed to him on November 25, 1926, to commission him to undertake the negotiations for handing back the concession that Belgium had in China. "One thing is certain," wrote the king, "and that is that unilateral treaties have had their day." "Must the Belgians", he asked, "go so far as to share in the unpopularity and, I would say, expose themselves to all the hate that the abuse of power is there constantly piling up? ... It is my profound conviction that we must make words of peace, of equity, of unselfishness heard. Belgium will become the greater thereby and will serve her own interests." This was the burden of my interview with the king, and the royal letter was expressed in the same terms that King Albert—that great statesman, who would not agree that loyalty, humility, and courage are handicaps for a sovereign—had used with me.

In the course of the audience, the warmth of my language had somewhat surprised the Minister Wei, who, as we left the palace, expressed to me the fear that I might have held the kind attention of the king too long. An hour later, I met the Count d'Aerschot, *Chef de Cabinet* to the king, at the Chinese legation. As I expressed to him regret for having perhaps wasted His Majesty's time, he exclaimed: "Not at all, not at all; the king is very glad to learn from you."

As the conclusion of the Peace Conference approached, several delegations made great efforts to discover what attitude the Chinese delegation was going to take. In the face of our reserve and of the firmness with which we maintained the elementary claim for the return to China of that part of Chinese territory which the Germans had occupied,[5] the Powers instructed their ministers at Beijing to bring pressure to bear on the Chinese government, that it might make common cause with all the Allies and that it might give me the order to sign. Impressed by these earnest representations, the government judged it imprudent to isolate itself by an ineffectual abstention, and it formally instructed me to sign the treaty.

For the first time in my career, I believed it to be my duty not to obey. Our country owed it to herself to consent no longer to letting herself be played with. I was not willing to sign my name yet again to unjust clauses, and I took it upon myself alone to refuse my signature. In evening of that same day, very late, when the closing session of the conference had come to an end several hours before, an entirely unexpected telegram from my government gave me the counter-order that I had had the boldness to carry out of my own accord.[6]

Providence, in which I have in so many circumstances recognized a helping hand, had once again manifestly

[5] That is, the return of Shandong and Jiaozhou Bay to Chinese control.—Ed.

[6] In the final text of the Treaty of Versailles, 1919, China is listed among the signatory powers but is the only nation without a signature from representatives.—Ed.

come to my assistance, and I had avoided, for my country's dignity and my own, being sucked into the backwash of that far too hesitant attitude of our rulers of that time.

At the time of my return to China, toward the end of 1919, at Shanghai, as I came off the boat, and at all the stations at which my train stopped, great popular demonstrations, cheering him who had refused to sign, testified to the Chinese government and to the foreign governments, that I had interpreted with perception the views of the country, which declared itself to be entirely with me.

The persistent hostility from abroad, from which I had had no respite, the lack of support from the government, and the absence of an exalted view and a persevering and coordinated campaign for renewing and reconstituting the forces of the nation convinced me that it was profitless for me to remain any longer at the helm of the Department for Foreign Affairs, or to continue to be made responsible before my country and before history for that accumulation of blunders before which so many others were withdrawing. My decision to leave the direction of Foreign Affairs came into force in December 1920. It marked the first stage in my secret desire to renounce political life.

No longer able to defend my country against her foreign foes, I devoted the last months I passed in China to doing what was in my power to meet the crying material needs of the populations of the various areas decimated by famine. I accepted the post of vice-director of the Office for Famine Relief. The documents that came into my hands showed me with a melancholy eloquence what becomes of the people of a great country when its governments fail in their duty over a long period.

In 1922, I left China. My wife's state of health demanded a period in Europe. We decided to spend it in Switzerland, where we owned a small property on the borders of Lake Maggiore.[7] I was very far from suspecting toward what future this voyage, since when I have not again seen my native country, was to lead me.

I encroach upon the narrative of my personal memories in order here to trace briefly the outline of my country's situation in the period after I had left public life.

China then knew a new danger, and perhaps the greatest of those that for nearly a century had been burdening her without respite. The population was more than ever longing to get to work in national reconstruction, and the country, scourged by the magnates, was within a hair's breadth of falling under a domination certainly as imperialist as that which Japan had promised herself and ceaselessly planned to impose upon us.

Since 1913, Dr. Sun Yat-sen had thought it his duty to oppose Mr. Yuan Shikai, who was already letting his ambition to the empire be seen. After the fall and death of Mr. Yuan, Dr. Sun returned from Japan, where he had been obliged to take refuge. The weakness and the failings of the government led him to found, at Canton in June 1917, a new government, which sought to gain control of the whole country.

This southern government encountered enormous difficulties, seeking in vain for technical assistance from abroad in the creation of an army worthy of the name, whose

---

[7] Luo Guang emphasizes that the cabin on Lake Maggiore was very modest and not a sign of wealth or opulence. The couple had purchased it earlier as a necessary site of convalescence for Lu when he needed rest from his diplomatic work, which was very taxing on his frail body.—Ed.

assistance was indispensable to it for the achievement of its aims. Its overtures in America, in Britain, and in Germany all met with refusals. Russia, on the other hand, with clever diplomacy, offered to help the Canton government, as much as and much more than it desired. Borodin became the high political adviser of that government.[8] He commanded a legion of civil and military experts and an army of propaganda agents whom the Soviets sent to us in order to gain a complete stranglehold on us, under the cover of the national renovation of which they professed themselves to be the keenest supporters.

By her policy of collaboration, which was the exact opposite of the abstentionist policy of the Western Powers and which seemed to provide the antidote to the Japanese policy of interference and occupation, the Russia of the Soviets obtained in 1923 precisely what in 1915, at the time when I was obliged to sign the Treaty of the Twenty-One Demands, we were, despite all, successful in refusing to Japan; that is to say, interference in the government, police control over our populations, and the right of propaganda throughout the country.

Meanwhile, the finest minds in all China worked to bring back unity. In January 1925, in response to an invitation of the government at Beijing, Dr. Sun Yat-sen had arrived in that city, animated by that personal disinterestedness that was always his and from which he legitimately expected the final success of his work of renovation. Alas, at the end of some weeks, a premature death carried him

---

[8] Lu uses "Southern Government" and "Canton Government" interchangeably. Sun's opposition government was centered in Guangzhou (anglicized in the past as "Canton"), which is the capital of China's southernmost province, Guangdong.—Ed.

off, on March 12, 1925, disclosing to the whole of China the greatness of the social and political task he had accomplished, the purity of his character, and the wisdom of his views.

In the moment of his death, the work of Dr. Sun Yatsen was in the danger that simultaneous civil war and political and military interference from Russia represented for it. This twofold danger was overcome in the space of three years by a statesman who is perhaps the greatest in the history of our country.

By his political genius, his clear vision, and his energy, Generalissimo Chiang Kai-Shek called a halt to the Russian game, destroyed the strength of Communism in China, and, in successive victories, succeeded, in the month of June 1928, in unifying the country, whose capital he transferred from Beijing to Nanjing, having the mortal remains of Dr. Sun Yat-sen triumphantly received in that city, and depositing them in the majestic mausoleum set up to the glory of the founder of the republic, indisputably recognized by the entire nation as the Father of the Fatherland.

The China of Generalissimo Chiang Kai-Shek was providentially to become the veritable New China, which the entire world today appreciates, loves, and acclaims, and which combines with all the strength of her glorious past the sure pledges of a magnificent future.

## Postscript: December 1944

The German occupation of Belgium, the rule of the Gestapo, and its incessant interference in private life did not permit me, last year, to put into writing my opinions about the present war, of which the beginnings are to be found in the Far East.[9]

On September 18, 1931, pursuing a policy that the Versailles Conference had encouraged, Japan took up arms again.[10] On July 7, 1937, the fire had all China in its grip.[11]

In vain did Chinese diplomatists utter loud cries: "The fire will not confine itself to our frontiers!" Everyone tried, so far as he could, to contradict them.

When, similarly, Hitler, in Germany, carried out the moral and material rearmament of his country, the alarm being general, the European Powers did nothing.

How is this to be explained? The incendiaries are at work; it is known, it is seen, and it is tolerated!

But what, then, is the duty of statesmen? Is it not to govern? Are statesmen free to be childish? When a fire is discovered, may they, like spoiled children, play with fire?... Fire has scorched the entire world.

This atrophy of the governmental sense is of a moral and spiritual order. It offers a clear field to veritable geniuses of cruelty; they become scourges of God.

The sacrifices, heroism, and suffering were and are unspeakable.

The nations will recover, provided that statesmen know how to forget their own selves, to educate the nations, to practice Justice and cause it to prevail.

---

[9] Lu here means World War II. The West tends to mark World War II as beginning with the German invasion of Poland in 1939. In the East, the beginning of the conflict is 1937, with the Marco Polo Bridge Incident and the subsequent Japanese invasion of China.—Ed.

[10] 1931 refers to the Japanese invasion of Manchuria (a territory in Northeast China), after which Japan established a puppet state.—Ed.

[11] In 1937, the Japanese invasion quickly captured major cities in China, including the infamous "Rape of Nanjing (Nanking)" in which the Japanese slaughtered Chinese civilians and surrendered soldiers en masse in Nanjing; estimates of the casualties are between 100,000 and 300,000.—Ed.

That requires the cooperation of all the spiritual forces of mankind.

May the statesmen of tomorrow, then, not commit the crime of filling themselves with pride, of "pasturing themselves",[12] of obscuring their moral and spiritual sense, and, in so doing, of losing the very principle of clearsightedness in government.

[12] Cf. Ezek 34. That chapter of Ezekiel is all of the highest political relevance.

# MY CHRISTIAN, RELIGIOUS, AND PRIESTLY VOCATION

*June 1943*

I HAVE kept for this third section a brief account of the spiritual progress that has been made within me through the course of my life and that includes my conversion to Catholicism and, eventually, my entry into the religious life and my accession to the priesthood.

But before tracing this progress, it seems to me that I owe a word of explanation to my fellow Catholics and, among them, especially to the young people, who often have difficulty in understanding the outlook of men and women whose education has not had contact with the life of Catholicism. Without this clarification, my account may leave unanswered a number of questions that they may be led to ask themselves.

When a man is born outside the Church, an acquaintance with Christian dogma is simply alien to him. He does not trouble about it, and it hardly enters his head that that subject might prove interesting.

Before that question can raise itself in his mind in its true proportions, some new factor must come into the familiar circumstances of his life, to focus his attention and little by little to direct it toward a field toward which his thought has had no tendency to direct itself. That new factor must be presented in the familiar setting of his thoughts and interests, or otherwise, unless by a miracle, it will produce no more than a passing impression on him, of which time and everyday preoccupations and the mere performance of the duties of his station will quickly blur the details and of which the memory will soon have no other importance than that of "general knowledge" in which one has neither any obligation nor any moral possibility of becoming interested.

You have read many stories of conversion to the Catholic Faith. There is as much variety among the descriptions of the ways by which God leads men toward Him as there is among their spiritual and moral characters. Each of them has a point of departure distinct from that of the others, and each follows an entirely personal road. One follows the way of a philosopher, in the search after truth; another the way of an artist, in the search after beauty; another the way of a man of affairs, in the search after well-being. Another the road of a Protestant pastor who, rising above controversies, penetrates in peace of intelligence and of heart to the meaning of revelation; another the road of a freethinker for whom every religious question is *a priori* superstition. Another the road of a man concerned with public affairs, out to remedy the misfortunes of one or another section of society; another the road of the statesman, who considers the general needs of a country, the needs that the state has to perceive and that include the life and well-being of the whole of civil society. These classifications doubtless do not represent watertight compartments; these various points of approach cut across one another; but whatever the road traversed, if one wishes to get to know the way by which a man approaches God, it is necessary to enter into his particular point of departure. *A fortiori* is that necessary if one has the task of helping him to travel along the road. And that is the A B C of every apostolate.

It was from the point of departure of a statesman that I approached the Church.

I told you in the first of these discussions how my master, Mr. Xu Jingcheng, had drawn my attention to that extraordinary fact, unique in the world, the Roman Church; and I spoke to you of his admiration for that universal spiritual government whose action had conferred on European society a moral strength that he desired for our own country. I described to you how he suggested that I should study the Christian religion very closely and that I should study most especially that Church which, being the most ancient, goes back to the origins of Christianity, and how he set me the task of enquiring into her and discovering her profound strength, in order to introduce that same strength into China.

It was, therefore, from the point of departure of a man of affairs, in search of well-being, that I studied and contemplated Holy Church, having as a guiding rule a principle that Jesus Christ Himself has given us: that it is by the fruits that you judge the tree.[1] I considered that that test alone, duly applied, amply sufficed to lead to conviction and to provide the foundation for a total adherence.

This preliminary observation seems to me necessary. I should be happy if it might stimulate among those young men preparing for the priesthood who will read these pages the desire to add to the study of theology that required for a knowledge and understanding of man—and of the man of the world; a knowledge that is proper to the priestly ministry, an understanding that God gives to profound minds, to children, and to the humble of heart. Animated by the virtues of faith and charity, that understanding is the first condition of every apostolate.

[1] Cf. Mt 7:20.

"My conversion is not a conversion; it is a vocation."

That reflection, which I find in my diary under the date of May 23, 1934, sums up the religious history of the Chinese politician who has been led by God, much more than by himself, toward the Church, toward the Benedictine Order, and toward the priesthood.

I am a Confucianist. When I was thirteen, my father placed me in the School of Foreign Languages in Shanghai, and I had not done the whole of the traditional Chinese classical studies. What matter! The intellectual and spiritual tradition of Confucianism, the cult of the Most High,[2] the practice of filial piety, the eagerness to give proof of virtue, in order to come to understand man better and to make progress in a practical manner in the acquisition of wisdom, all that makes up the spirit of the Chinese race since the time of Yao, of Shun, and of Yu, the contemporaries of Abraham, in submission to the master of ten thousand generations, Confucius, and to that other great philosopher, Mencius—by all this I have ceaselessly desired to be molded and nourished, all the more because I am not a doctor or a licentiate or a bachelor in letters; and because I have spent almost all my life abroad, often very isolated in the midst of the varying surroundings in which I have found myself and having to carry on a constant fight for my country, whose past, present, and future were the object of every derision and of every contempt.

The making of these moral efforts had no other object than that of obedience to my duty as a man, and I found the reward for it in the filial joy given by the duty itself, whose accomplishment made it possible for me to be not

---

[2] That is, the worship of *Shangdi* 上帝, "The Emperor on High". *Shangdi* was the primary deity of the Shang dynasty and is frequently mentioned in Confucian classics such as the *Book of the Odes* (*Shijing*).—Ed.

too unworthy of Heaven and not to dishonor my country, my parents, and my master.

You know to what extent Chinese literary studies have been slandered, and how much it has been said that they stultify the minds of the students, and, moreover, that Confucianism itself was an obsolete system that had disintegrated and could not stand up to modernization.[3] Those who have used and those who use this language have confused Confucianism with the distorted and pharisaical use that has been made of it by certain people, and they have not perceived that, whatever may be the modernization that was necessary, the old Chinese system of schooling had at least the merit of not teaching the exercise of reading without teaching at the same time the exercise of judgment; for the man who knows how to read and does not know how to judge is in danger of laying open his mind, his memory, and his heart to whatever the first-comer wishes to plant there.

In spite of some appearances, the Chinese classical studies offer much to compare with European studies of the

---

[3] The precise critique of Chinese education to which Lu is responding is unclear. On the one hand, his comments might fit the critiques of the New Culture Movement in China, which alleged that the old education system prioritizing memorization and recitation of classical texts—and largely eschewing study of modern Western sciences—was an obstacle to modernization. He could also, however, mean general Western critiques of Chinese education popular in Europe at the time, which saw Chinese education as hopelessly unmodern. For example, Arthur Moule noted Western assumptions of the Chinese as an unsophisticated and uneducated people in his *The Chinese People: A Handbook on China* (London: Society for Promoting Christian Knowledge, 1914), 260. Moule, who defends Chinese education, explicitly defends the practice of memorization and bemoans its abandonment in the education of his own time, both East and West (262). At the very least, such passages indicate a general spirit of critique for traditional Chinese education based on classic texts in both Europe and China during Lu's lifetime.—Ed.

humanities. If today in Europe a man confined himself to studying Latin and Greek, he would be inevitably a backward man. But if, in no matter what country, a man is ignorant of and despises the intellectual and literary foundations of civilization, he is very near to being no longer civilized, and the question is then presented of knowing not only in what degree he can *know* man, but in what degree he *is* a man.

The Confucianist spirit led me to see the evident superiority of Christianity, as three centuries ago it led the Minister of State Paul Xu; and that without regard to the personal shortcomings of Christians—or rather, in the very field of human qualities and shortcomings. The Confucianist spirit led me to recognize the superiority, so very plain, of the Holy Roman Church, holding a treasure from which, from century to century, the believer draws riches ancient and new; a living treasure that, from century to century, increases and bears fruit.

At the center of Catholic worship, we find the celebration of a sacrifice of which the august character infinitely surpasses all the sacrifices that, in whatever religion, have sought to express the relations between man and God and to render glory to God.

It was instituted by Jesus Christ on the eve of His death. It commemorates the crucifixion of Jesus. It is the mysterious renewing of it. Daily all over the world the celebration of the sacrifice of the Mass groups round more than three hundred thousand altars those to whom the death of the Lord appears as the principle of their spiritual life. Has ever a man died who knew, in the souls of hundreds of millions of human beings, a resurrection so profound, so enduring, so intimate, so renewing?

That spiritual life, which flows from the sacrifice of Jesus Christ upon the Cross, the Church manifests and dispenses to her faithful by the ministry of the seven sacraments instituted by Jesus Christ to signify the gift of grace and to dispense it. By this sacramental ministry, the Church gives life and sustenance to man from the cradle to the grave, giving a constant maternal support to the human person and, through that person, to the family and to all society. This fact of the Mass and the seven sacraments alone calls for observation and reflection and compels admiration and respect.

However little informed a man may be in religious matters, if he comes at a given moment of his existence to leave the setting of that ignorance and of the limitation that it involves, he enters upon horizons that have nothing of fantasy about them and that are immense. He is given an insight into the condition of the human race on earth in an incomparably more profound and more living light, happier, greater, and more peaceful. To resolve the apparent contradictions of human life, it is no longer necessary for him to take refuge in subjective ideas; for he has the power to embrace the whole of life as it is, its worth and its mediocrity, its weakness and its strength, its suffering and its joy, its freedom and its dependence, its misery, its sin, and its sanctity, its brevity, and its immortality. And this life appears to him then unified by the sanctity of its origin, which is God, and by the glory of its final end, which is, it also, the One True God.

The attentive consideration of the maternal and social character of the Universal Church leads to a search for an understanding of a spiritual institution so grandly conceived and instituted in a manner at once divine and human.

It is that which Mr. Xu Jingcheng had perceived, half a century ago. He did not believe himself to be in a position personally to take the many steps that are necessary for a Chinese, overcoming the frontiers of civilizations and languages very distant from one another, to feel at ease in an institution of which, today still, the external appearance, Latin and Western, does not completely express the internal and profound universality.

I have spoken to you of the influence of Mr. Xu's remarks on the course of my observation, my research, and my thought.

Confucianism, whose standards of moral life are so profound and so beneficial, finds in the Christian revelation and in the existence and life of the Catholic Church the most illustrious justification of all, human and immortal, that it possesses, and it finds there at the same time the fulfillment of moral light and moral strength, which solves the problems before which our sages have had the humility to draw back, understanding that it does not belong to man to penetrate the mystery of Heaven and that it is necessary, in venerating the Providence of Heaven, to wait until, if He deigns to do so, the Creator Himself reveals Himself.

But what, then, is the ambition of the Church, and what is her secret? Whence came to her that interior strength that can, at this point, convince and "convert" a Far Eastern? How has it been possible for a bridge to be built between her and me? How is that bridge to be built between her and the whole yellow[4] world, in order that we all may be able to feel the divine order of this institution, of her doctrine, of her morality, and of her very existence, of which the eminent superiority, *de facto* and *de jure*, is universal?

How can Christianity, which has grown up in the Western world and, while always distinguishing itself from it,

---

[4] Lu is accommodating to racial language used at the time in Europe in order to describe those of East Asian descent. Today, of course, this language would be considered to be in poor taste. However, it is worth noting that in Chinese, the color yellow (*huang* 黃) is a propitious and fortunate color, meaning Lu could embrace it for positive connotations as well.—Ed.

has penetrated it to the extent of being identified with it—how can Christianity be in a position to become identified in the same way with the Eastern world and to retain, in again thoroughly imbuing it, her own identity?

The unity, the universality, the disinterested ambition and the secret of the Church find their principle, of necessity, in the origin of that institution.

I should like to say to my countrymen: "Read, then, the Gospels, the Acts of the Apostles, the Epistles; read the history of the persecutions of the first centuries of the Church and the story of her martyrs; take all the pages of the history of the Church, including those blemished by the weakness or the malice of certain men who lived otherwise than they spoke or preached; take also those countless pages wherein Christian charity has been practiced and is being practiced with a tireless and so often heroic maternal solicitude. Distinguish between what is of man and what is of God, and you will end with a social fact absolutely superior and unique. Perhaps, then, you will ask yourself the question: 'Has the Creator here revealed Himself?'"

Faith is a gift of God, but the act of faith presupposes information, an investigation. Observe the work of the Church in men's consciences and her vitality in the fields of family and social, civic, and political life. Jesus Christ said to His disciples, "But seek first his kingdom and his righteousness, and all these things shall be yours as well."[5] Weigh those words; they show a sure way to that summit of human grandeur and greatness of mind that is the millenary ideal of Confucianism: "To bring peace to the universe."

I repeat: independently of the personal deficiencies of those who are members of the Church or of those who hold one or another position of authority in her, independently of the errors and the faults that they may commit

[5] Mt 6:33.

in their daily life, is it imaginable that such an organization ought not to be studied from within, examined and thoroughly investigated, by every reasonable man and ought not to be respected and desired—without the least prejudice to the full liberty of consciences—by every society solicitous for the well-being of its members and by every state zealous for the human greatness of its citizens? What an incomparable assistance, what a remission of labor and of responsibility for the civil authority, it is to see such a work accomplished in the midst of families and populations; and how greatly ought not that authority to exert its every effort to ensure that an institution of such grandeur, of such rich fertility, all of whose services are known to be disinterested, might flourish in the midst of its peoples and for the greatest good of all!

That is how, little by little, freely and slowly, the Confucianist tradition and the grace of God led me to enter into a more and more intimate relation with Christianity and with the Catholic Church.

I believe that in the development of the thoughts that, day by day, drew me toward the Church, I remained entirely independent of all external influence; and I have already told you how my wife, that exemplary Christian, had made that approach easier *by not speaking to me about it*; if she had spoken to me about it, above all if she had insisted, I should have recoiled; for the very nature of the religious act demands above all that it should be freely made. God shows man his duties, but man remains free to obey or disobey. It is ordained that man shall pray the Most High to enlighten him and to give him strength, to perceive his duty and to carry it out.

All this took place within me in evident fulfillment of a divine Providence, to which I received the grace to endeavor to respond.

That is why I said to you above, "My conversion is not a conversion": it is not I who was converted, under some external influence or by some personal design. "My conversion is a vocation": God led me, and He called me. My task for myself has, then, been extremely simple: it was enough for me to recognize what I saw, what events and circumstances and the grace of God plainly showed me, and, to this constant and clear vocation, to respond by fulfilling the first duty of conscience, which is to obey God. It is by obedience to the truth and to duty that I have been unable to do anything else but to become a Christian and a Catholic. May God alone be praised for it!

You ask yourselves a question: How did the principles of Catholic dogma, at first sight intricate and involved, appear to me? How did I give my adhesion and my faith to that dogma?

In proportion as I studied Holy Church did I have confidence in her and did I believe. In believing I advanced, and at each step of the way I saw the light increase and I felt that love was swelling within me.

As I have already told you, Confucianists distrust certain kinds of intellectual speculation that, when it comes to the problem of life, are rather *jeux d'esprit* than a search after truth and wisdom. Before the mystery of the hereafter and all that it means, Confucianism adopts a personal attitude of respect and reserve, for it recognizes that that is indeed the domain where the imagination runs freely to the creation of phantoms and idols at every turn.

Having recognized in the Church a human and a superhuman character, a spiritual and moral coordination and balance that are unique, an influence for good that is inexhaustible and a setting in which spiritual health and heroism spontaneously flourish, I believed in her divine origin, and I sought, in being drawn toward her, to take in with an eager eye everything that my eyes could see or discover or penetrate; but at the same time I was quite resolved not to judge *a priori*, not to make up my mind in advance about higher things that require consideration and reflection, competence and impartiality, and that I was scarcely beginning to know. My wife, in a somewhat summary judgment, told me that I had the faith of a charcoal-burner. At least I had tried to avoid presumption; and experience has taught me that I was not mistaken.

It was in entering the monastery that I really approached Catholic dogma, in the first place by prayer and, more especially, by the prayer of the liturgy and by the teaching it gives.

It makes the divine ordering of human life live and live again, and it leads, step by step, to the very center of the redemptive work of Jesus Christ. It reveals that work in the life of Christ, in the life of the Church, and in the souls of the saints: the liturgy of the living and the admirable liturgy of the dead. Let it be said in passing: instead of discussing the Chinese rites, why did they not show to all Chinese the incomparable liturgy of the dead, which is perhaps only displayed in all its marvelous and sober grandeur in the churches and cloisters of the monastic Orders?

The liturgy of the Mass, the Divine Office, and the sacraments led me to know the person of Jesus Christ, the Son of the Living God, Who reconciles man with God, Who has given us the Spirit of God by which, a thing well-nigh inconceivable, we become children of the Most High, from Whom comes all fatherhood and Whom we ourselves can call "our Father".

I approached the Passion of Jesus Christ, and I was enlightened on this subject by an exchange of letters with one of my eminent compatriots, who thereby became a master in the Christian life for me, namely, Father Ma Liang, who, as you well know, at the age of ninety-five, universally venerated, has translated and published in the Chinese language the most beautiful words of our Divine Redeemer. In my maternal language did I approach my Savior and the Savior of the human race.

That meditation on the life, the work, and the moral and physical Passion of Jesus Christ was the strength and the support thanks to which, at the age of fifty-six, I was able to initiate myself into a manner of life entirely new to me: the life of a Catholic monk.

I meditated on the Gospel on my own behalf and on behalf of my country. In its light I lived again through all the insults that the Chinese people had suffered and suffer still, whose feebleness has been the jest of the world for a hundred years. I lived again, also, very peacefully, through all the humiliations that so many foreigners—and foreigners often of very doubtful moral or intellectual worth— had inflicted on me at will, for the sole reason that I was a Chinese. These humiliations of my country, of my countrymen, and of my own person had not left any bitterness in me at all. In the light from the On High, they became for me, still more than in the past, a source of strength and of life, of love and of resurrection.

All our sufferings find their consolation, their justification, and their solution in the redemptive work of Jesus Christ, to which we are able to bring our modest contribution. Our trials, then, disappear: God, Who is our Father, makes Himself the Guarantee and the Reward of those who choose the narrow path leading upward toward Him. And those trials become a source of life and of happiness for us and for those whom we love. I should like to quote here those magnificent words of a French woman of letters of whom I shall shortly speak: *Toute âme qui s'élève élève le monde* (every soul that rises, raises the world)."[6]

This calls for a daily effort in an atmosphere of interior courage, of spiritual joy and lightheartedness. In making that effort, I was sustained by the dispositions in which I had decided on my entry into the cloister after the death of my wife. I was also encouraged by the moving profession of Christian faith that His Majesty King Albert then condescended to address to me and by the paternal benevolence, so many times repeated, with which His Holiness Pope Pius XI overwhelmed me up to the time of his death. I entered into a Catholicism profoundly lived, and I saw with great clarity the benefit that my country—I am certain of it—will receive from the development there to which the Catholic Church is called. Moreover, I had before my eyes, here in Belgium, one of the most remarkable examples of the support that the Church can give to a nation in peril, in the person of Cardinal Mercier, whose recent death displayed his glory and who, in an enforced absence of the government's authority, had been, in tragic circumstances, for four years the soul of his country.

All this was going on within me while I was living in the Benedictine Monastery, at first in the novitiate among my very young brethren under the direction of Father Novice Master, Dom Gabriel Eggermont, and then in the community under the direction of Reverend Father Abbot, Dom Théodore Nève, in a family house, with all the profound sense that that word "family" carries, of mutual obligations, of support, of respect and affection, and with all its meaning of simplicity, of reality, and, I dare to say, of realism and worldliness.

---

[6] Elisabeth Leseur, *Journal et Pensées de chaque jour* (Paris: de Gigord, 1927), 31.

*Formal portrait of Lu Zhengxiang in diplomatic regalia.*
*Chinese diplomat for the Qing Empire. 1907.*

*Formal portrait of Lu Zhengxiang in diplomatic attire. Republic of China's plenipotentiary at Berne, Switzerland. 1925.*

*Group photo with Yuan Shikai (front, center), Lu Zhengxiang (two persons away from Yuan Shikai), and other members of the international diplomatic community. Republic of China. 1915.*

*Xu Jingcheng (1845–1900), Lu's diplomatic mentor.*

*Lu Zhengxiang and his beloved wife, Berthe* née *Bovy of Belgium.*

*Group photo taken at Saint Andrew's Monastery, Belgium, before Lu Zhengxiang's entrance into the abbey as a Benedictine monk. 1927. (Lu Zhengxiang, first row, center.)*

*Group photo taken at Saint Andrew's Monastery, Belgium, after Lu Zhengxiang's entrance into the abbey as a Benedictine monk. 14 January 1928. (Lu Zhengxiang, first row, second from the left.)*

*Br. Pierre-Célestin Lu, O.S.B. (Lu Zhengxiang), before his
ordination to the priesthood at Saint Andrew's Monastery,
Belgium. 29 June 1935.*

*Br. Pierre-Célestin Lu, O.S.B. (Lu Zhengxiang), at his
ordination to the priesthood at Saint Andrew's Monastery,
Belgium. 29 June 1935.*

*Photo taken of Fr. Pierre-Célestin Lu, O.S.B., at Saint Andrew's Monastery, Belgium, with a brother monk. Ca. 1940.*

*Formal portrait of Fr. Pierre-Célestin Lu, O.S.B., at Saint Andrew's Monastery, Belgium, before his election to titular abbot by Pope Pius XII. 1 August 1946.*

陸
公
微
祥
遺
像

*Formal portrait of Dom Pierre-Célestin Lu, O.S.B., at Saint Andrew's Monastery, Belgium, after his election to titular abbot by Pope Pius XII. 10 August 1946.*

*Abbot Pierre-Célestin Lu, O.S.B., reading the Gospel in his office.*

*Abbot Pierre-Célestin Lu, O.S.B., with his miter and crozier at his installation as titular abbot of the Abbey of Saint Peter of Ghent. 10 August 1946.*

*Formal portrait of Abbot Pierre-Célestin Lu, O.S.B., with his miter and crozier after his installation as titular abbot of the Abbey of Saint Peter of Ghent. 10 August 1946.*

Then, after this entry into the monastic life, my abbot called me to the priesthood. That appeal was strangely confirmed by an act of my Confucianist friends, who, not being Christians, presented me with the chalice that they wished to see me raise toward Heaven and the chasuble that I had to put on to approach the altar. This gift came to me in the spring of 1933, at a time when access to the priesthood seemed to me very far away....

This was a drama for me.

I do not speak of the difficulties that, from the age of fifty-six to sixty-four, were presented by the study of the Latin language, of which I was totally ignorant, and of theology. That acquisition demanded a laborious effort, of which, at that age, the apprehension alone was enough to bring on fatigue. The real problem was very different; it was of the moral order. I asked myself the question: "How could I, I, become a priest? How could I daily present myself before the face of God as a representative of mankind?" A thousand times I felt myself incapable of responding to this vocation, and a thousand times I thought that at my age, and after the career I had followed, too much was being asked of me. I obeyed; and it was necessary for me—for how long, and how many times a day!—to force myself to obey.

But truly it was God who took me into His arms. My confessor, Dom Étienne Tillieux, of pious and regretted memory, had said to me: "When you are a priest, you will be completely changed." Five days after my ordination, which was conferred on me on June 29, 1935, by the archbishop, whose person symbolized for me the whole Church of Christ, the whole Church of China, and the whole Church of Rome, I was compelled to recognize it, and that day I made this confidence to one of my brethren, who, like me, has never forgotten it: "I am changed."

And nevertheless, after that, once I was a priest, I was filled with fear and—I must say it—with trembling. It was a terrible struggle with myself to dare to approach, every day, myself, the Omnipotent. The Lord came to my assistance. When in November 1935 pneumonia came to deprive me for forty days of the possibility of celebrating Holy Mass—forty days during which Communion was brought to me daily—the Lord deigned to enlighten me and to make me understand that, in my anxiety to do my duty, I had made the gifts of His bounty one-sided, and that, fearing Him as a Master, I had not understood that He is truly a Father. Since that time, seeing clearly that I offered the Sacrifice to God, our Father, I no longer feared to approach the altar. And the daily Mass became, in the composure of the monastery and its cloister, the great act of all the day, the unique and very simple act, face to face with God, in my capacity, in my office as an "other Christ", a priest.

Today, after eight years in the priesthood, Providence seems to lead me to the apostolate. That is going on now; it becomes more marked from day to day. How has this new desire been able to take possession of me, at an age when it is not at all usual to prepare one's self for action?

The cry of my country in the sufferings of a war that has now lasted for nearly six years; the lofty dignity with which the Chinese government and people hold up their heads before a tempest of steel and fire, still so ill-equipped, beating against an army; the rampart of human bodies raised by the heroism of hundreds of thousands of my countrymen, who, under the leadership of an admirable leader, have known how to prefer death to subjection; the moral victory by which China has taken her place in the first rank of the nations of the world—all these expressions of the patriotic ideal to which from my youth I have dedicated my life could not fail to warm my heart and to give me, with the help of God, that renewal of physical health and moral vigor that is in itself a sign from Providence and an invitation to action.

All this encouragement, all these examples touched the priest's heart within me and awoke those new and greater gifts for which my age has been nothing of an obstacle and which created in me a new moral strength and, verily, a new youth. I had had that feeling of renewal very clearly ever since I entered the cloister. On the day of my admission into the novitiate, January 14, 1928, wishing to give publicly a new sign of my faithfulness to the dear companion of my life, I drew up a second memorial card, which I concluded by thanking her for having been "my guide" and for having "shown the way in which God has deigned to accord to His sheep a new life, a new youth, and a new career." After seventeen years of life in the cloister, that career was to know a new beginning.

Now began the Second World War; since 1931, it had been preparing in the Far East, and from China it had spread even to Europe.

When, in May 1940, the storm broke in Belgium, when the gravely wounded poured into and, six to eight hundred at a time, filled the cloisters of the Abbey of Saint Andrew, in a magnificent expression and moving witness to the heroism of the Belgian army, the vocation to the apostolate presented itself to my conscience in a well-nigh imperative form, and what had for so long been a desire appeared to me as a duty and became an earnest wish, a determination.

One opportunity was enough for this new vocation to be defined and to enter upon a first phase of realization.

On March 25, 1942, the Community of Saint Andrew received the order to evacuate the abbey buildings, requisitioned by the occupying power in order there to accommodate a part of the German army. This time I had the feeling that I was no longer able to delay. Since the Lord made me, provisionally, leave the cloister, it was because He intended, considering my age, with a divine wisdom, Himself to direct me toward the good to be done, toward apostolic action. The four months that I passed at Bruges in the hospitable house of Baron Ryelandt allowed me to grasp more clearly still what Providence expected of me. With the full approval of my superiors, whose secret hope I was assuredly fulfilling, I began the ministry of speech—at first, modestly, before the religious community of the English Convent at Bruges; then at Antwerp, in the parish of the Saint-Esprit, before an audience of three hundred people, members of Catholic Action; and after that in the Grands Séminaires of Bruges and Malines and before the various audiences to which Providence led me, giving me an awareness of the priestly ministry that God had bestowed on me and a preparation for the day when I should have to bear witness to Christ before my countrymen in my own country.

There is the sequence of my vocation: to the Christian and the Catholic life; then from the condition of a simple believer to that of a religious and a monk, to that of a priest; of a priest who, in his seventies, has entered the apostolate.

May I take up again the thread of my philosophical and religious thought?

I am a Confucianist because that moral philosophy, in which I was brought up, profoundly penetrates the nature of man and traces clearly his line of conduct toward his Creator, toward his parents, and toward his fellows, individuals, and society.

I am a Christian and a Catholic because Holy Church, prepared from the beginning of mankind, founded by Jesus Christ, the Son of God, divinely enlightens and sustains the soul of man and gives the conclusive response to all our highest thoughts, to all our best desires, to all our aspirations, to all our needs.

This veritable light sheds her rays upon our origin and our destiny, on the meaning of our worldly lives, on our redemption, and on our end.

The Christian and Catholic Church, the Holy Roman Church, is the divine, marvelous, and indispensable complement to all that I possessed, to all that I anticipated, sought, and desired, and to the fundamental institutions of my people.

She is the gift of God, Who deigned to love man and to confer upon him the immense benefit of destining him to become His child.

But, as I have said to you, my conversion was not a conversion; it was a vocation. It was not, *in the first place*, the result of an awakening and a personal effort of my intelligence and my will. It was not I who planned the route; it was not I who marked it out. I saw the route; God gave me the light; I knew the love God has for us, and I believed in it. All I did was to try to respond to the Light and to the Love. In all the feebleness of my intelligence and my heart, with His aid, I tried to walk. And by His grace, I found that I had made the journey.

As I have said already, it was at the end of the year 1920 that my political career in fact came to an end.

In that same year, 1920, I fulfilled a long-standing duty of filial piety. I acquired, at the gates of Beijing, at the crest of some rising ground, about half a hectare of land facing the Catholic cemetery of Zhalan, and I devoted the greater part of it to the arrangement of a garden, in the center of which I had built a chapel whose crypt was suited to the reception of the mortal remains of my paternal grandmother and of my venerated father and mother. In a corner of this garden, I had reserved a place for a vault that would become a resting-place for my wife and me. The main entry into the garden was so disposed as to face the glorious tombs of the Reverend Fathers Matteo Ricci, Adam Schall, and Ferdinand Verbiest, who are buried at Zhalan. The choice of this burial place and its disposition in themselves express all my thought.

On November 14, 1920, the bodies of my grandmother and my parents were solemnly taken there.

I intended to build, eventually, on the second part of the property, a villa where my wife and I planned to end our days. This villa I had in advance called "Mu Lu: cottage of veneration"—cottage where I was going to live in a sentiment of recognition of all that I had received from God through my parents and, above all, of the benefit of life and of education, which every man owes to his father and mother.[7]

I little thought that Providence was going to dispose of my future quite otherwise and was going to transport my "Mu Lu" from Zhalan, where I had put it, to a Benedictine monastery in Belgium, there to render thanks to God for all that I received from Him through my parents and for all that He gives ceaselessly to us all through Jesus Christ.[8]

[7] Lu used a clever pun in naming his cottage, since the Chinese word for grave is *mù* 墓 and a word for honor and admiration is *mù* 慕 (the name of the cottage is *mulu* 慕廬).—Ed.

[8] When he says his cottage was "transported", Lu refers to the fact that he called his room at Saint Andrew's *mulu* 慕廬.—Ed.

In 1922, as I have already related, my wife's health left much to be desired. We decided to leave for Europe and to settle on the shores of Lake Maggiore, in our Locarno villa. During my period at The Hague, in 1908, I had bought this very agreeable *pied-à-terre*, and every year, so long as circumstances permitted, we went to spend a month there.

As we were staying at Locarno, I received a proposal from my government, suggesting that I should take over the direction of our legation in Paris. I declined this offer. But some time afterward, seeing the level of French War Bonds, which I had bought in large numbers, sink considerably, I was compelled to request a return to my profession. I particularly asked for a post of the second rank. My request coincided with the government's desire to promote Mr. Wang Yongbo, our Minister at Bern, who was to be nominated for Tokyo. I became his successor, and I recruited for the staff of the legation at Berne Mr. Raymond Wang, my predecessor's son. During the four years in which I represented China in Switzerland, I established relations marked by the most cordial sympathy with many members of the Swiss government—I should like here to recall in particular Mr. Motta, minister for foreign affairs, and Mr. Musy, finance minister, who became my very dear friends—with several of my colleagues in the diplomatic corps, and with a number of the distinguished personalities of that beautiful country of Switzerland, so justly proud of her national independence and of the liberal character of her institutions.

We had not been long at Bern when God dealt me a very hard blow. My wife was struck down with cerebral congestion, and it soon became evident that her illness, which would be long, no longer offered hope of her recovery.[9] God was thwarting, with His blessed hand, all that we had ourselves for so long planned.

My first duty was to return to my beloved invalid some small part of all the love and all the giving of herself in which she had united herself with me, sharing with the courage of "a daughter and a granddaughter of officers"— that is her own phrase—the risks and the dangers that, in the course of my public career, had been so often multiplied. I devoted myself entirely to her, and in this labor of love, of which the outcome was not in question, I saw presenting itself to me, in a practical manner, the suggestion that the Minister Xu Jingcheng had made to me thirty years before. If the Lord should take away my wife, I would enter a religious house in Europe, and that act would combine two loyalties: to the consort who would have left me and to the testament of my master, recommending me to go right through to the end with my "Europeanization" and to make my own that interior life of religion that, like him, I had felt to be the true secret strength of all that is best and most enduring in Europe.

I was casting about for a means of telling the dear companion of my life of the gravity of her condition and of the form that I intended to give to my loyalty to her when I discovered the recently published works of Madame Elisabeth Leseur, whose husband had become Father Leseur, with whom I was later to form an intimate friendship. My wife and I read together the *Journal et Pensées de chaque jour* (journal of thoughts for each day). This reading made it possible for our two hearts to understand one another, to penetrate into one another, more deeply than ever, without our having any need of long explanations. We were

---

[9] Modern medicine refers to this condition as apoplexy, which involves a stroke in some instances.—Ed.

both, she and I, to strive to follow the example, she of Elisabeth Leseur, and I of her husband.[10] Meanwhile, I tried every means of relieving the invalid and, if possible, of obtaining her cure. In 1925 I made a pilgrimage to Rome in her name. The nuncio to Bern, Msgr. Maglione, later secretary of state to His Holiness, had the great kindness to request an audience of the Sovereign Pontiff, Pius XI, for me. I approached the Holy Father in a spirit of interior piety, venerating in his person the Vicar of Jesus Christ. The audience lasted more than half an hour. The pope blessed my dear sick wife, to whom I took from the eternal city a new joy, serenity, and peace. At the hour of her departure from this earth, the nuncio personally gave the Apostolic Benediction to my dear dying one. I retain an inexpressible gratitude to His Eminence Cardinal Maglione.[11]

On the very day of my wife's death, April 16, 1926, I began to put into execution the plan with which the Lord had inspired me, and I begged Father de Munnynck, a professor at the University of Fribourg, whose spiritual direction my wife had desired to receive, to be so good as to give it to me instead. After some months, I confided to him my plan of becoming a religious. Father de Munnynck concurred, and shortly afterward he put me in touch with the abbot of Saint Andrew's, near Bruges, in Belgium.

In the month of June 1927, having laid the body of my dear dead wife in a vault that I had had made at Brussels, in

---

[10] Elisabeth Leseur had been a committed, devout Catholic and wife of Felix Leseur, who was a medical doctor and leader of atheist movements in France. Leseur's testimony to the faith eventually led Felix to convert after his beloved wife's death, and he became a Dominican priest. Lu met Fr. Leseur after the latter gave a talk in Bern shortly before Berthe's passing.—Ed.

[11] Very prematurely, on August 22, 1944, Cardinal Maglione was called to God.

the cemetery at Laeken—chosen by me because it is near the tombs of the Belgian Royal Family—I came to spend Whitsuntide at the Abbey of Saint Andrew. In the evening of Whit Tuesday, I asked and obtained from Father Abbot admission as a postulant of this monastery. According to the advice of Father de Munnynck, I had asked to become a Benedictine Oblate. When I finally arrived at the abbey, on July 5th, there to spend at first three months in the guesthouse, Father Abbot proposed that I should go one step farther and seek canonical entry into the novitiate.[12] I reconciled myself to his invitation, and it is thanks to it and to that first step that today, without my having ever previously expected it, I see myself clothed with the priestly dignity and office.

I noted, a good deal later, toward 1931, the feelings with which, at the death of the companion of my life, I addressed myself to the religious life. I will allow myself to give here a brief extract from those notes:

> It is here, purely and simply, a matter of something very ordinary, that may be very common and very general: that is, that two partners who were not born either on the same day or at the same hour die together at the same minute, at the same second indicated by Providence.
>
> Our understanding of each other is, then, extended into the hereafter.
>
> She has carried my religious life into her grave, and I have carried her eternal life into my retreat.
>
> What is there remaining for us to say to one another, to suggest to one another, to ask of one another? We have

---

[12] The life of the oblate is one committed to the rules of life governing a particular community, but without vows. By entering the novitiate, Lu was introduced into the full monastic life and permanent vows, including (typically) preparation for the priesthood.—Ed.

given to each other all that God has given us to exchange between us: body against body, heart against heart, soul against soul, the religious life against eternal life. Yes; death has separated us, but the religious life has united us a second time, and forever. She watches over me; I pray with and for her. She looks at me from above; I admire her from below. Between us, no distance has ever existed. Today, one more bond unites us more closely than ever; our communion. Oh, my dear life's friend, for me thou art not dead; thou livest. But I, I am dead, and have well died, for thee!

It was difficult for my countrymen—even, and above all, for my best friends—to understand by what inspiration I had decided for disappearance, for death to the world, even to becoming a monk in a Catholic monastery, in a foreign land, in Europe; and they asked themselves whither an act so unexpected by them might well lead me.

It took several years before the fears that sympathy aroused in them were quietened; they were concerned for my health, which they knew to be delicate; a setback in health might have been irremediable. Several among them had the friendliness and the courage to tell me of the anxiety and the solicitude that I was causing them. I was deeply moved by this. The loyalty with which they have continued and multiplied, even to this day, the signs of their affectionate interest in me have not ceased to be a source of strength and joy and precious encouragement for me.

The general feeling of my countrymen on the subject of my entry into an abbey in Belgium is very easy to understand. Public opinion and society in China were, in fact, far from sharing, on the subject of the Christian religion, the opinions of Mr. Xu, that great precursor, and my own opinions; and they attributed to an excess of sorrow a decision that appeared to them as an aberration. When my friends in China learned that my health, far from becoming worse, was much improving and that my love for my country, of which they knew the character and the depth, was still growing; when they saw that, if I had died at the same time as my wife, it was to live again with her, and to live again immediately, in order to contribute to the spiritual strength of my country, they changed their minds; and my faithful old servant, who used to go from time to time to pay them his respects and to give them my news, gained now a very different opinion on their part: "Your master has done well."

One word more, to the glory of our Lord Jesus Christ, to conclude this account and to show the way in which, from my childhood and through my whole career, God has guided me; to show how, by His grace and, if one may say so, without my having been aware of it, I have allowed myself to be guided by Him. I find these lines on that same page of my journal, for May 23, 1934, whose opening phrase I gave you at the beginning of this discourse:

> My conversion is not a conversion; it is a vocation. It is a conversion made of trials and a conversion made of graces.
>
> Trials are reserved for the friends of God, and these trials are graces—my birth and, eight years later, in circumstances equally poignant, the death of my mother; my marriage "boycotted"; the death of my father without my being able to help him; the execution of my master; my home remaining childless; finally, the last trial of my private life, the death of my wife. This last trial, this also, so hard as it was to bear, was yet a grace, by which God called to Himself my life's companion.
>
> I was not seeking after the True Light.
>
> I have simply been called by God; and it was only after the death of my wife that I recognized the true character of trials: a character of grace.

By the side of these trials of my private life, God filled my career with the highest tasks that a man can carry. But these tasks likewise had been preceded by the most hard and the most constant humiliations. And my public offices never ceased to be fulfilled in the midst of the most unjust humiliations of my dear country.

Until my appointment as a minister, I had always been treated with great arrogance by high officials, as one who, not having passed the official examinations, was almost an intruder. I was so used to it that in the end I no longer even noticed it. In the eyes of my equals, I seemed then as a veritable sycophant. My submission seemed to them to be an attitude of abasement and flattery. That lasted fourteen years. And these charges, these humiliations, these mortifications, these graces, these trials, these honors, and all my tasks have always been given to me, or, rather, have always been imposed upon me, almost against my will. I have always been afraid to accept the situations to which I have been called, and I have never ceased to say to myself, "I am not prepared."

I must say this: during the whole course of my life, God has caused to be said to me through my superiors that which He has wished to make me hear, so that, learning it from Him through voices of authority, I was not dismayed at disappointments. When the disappointments came, I was forewarned.

A conversion—what is it? It is a search for the True Light. But I, I have gone forward without knowing it. Truly I have searched for nothing, not for light, not for happiness. I have simply striven to do my duty.

After the death of my wife, I felt myself isolated. *That was the only time I have sought for something— for a retreat.* At that time I began to pray, to seek, with the idea of entering a House of the good God. It was a search based on the advice of Mr. Xu: "Rely on yourself, and do not rely on anyone else." Based also on what my father had said to me during his lifetime: "Rely on God." I had then no longer a father, a master, or a wife. From then onward, I had to rely solely upon God and upon myself.

And the good God caused me to go forward ...

I entered the religious life. Doubtless all beginnings are difficult. The Lord ceaselessly asked me the question: "Have you sufficient compliance to do all that I wish you to do?" What could I reply? "I will strive to have the compliance of Saint Joseph ..."

In the last phase of my life, since the question of my accession to the priesthood arose, I have been, this time, fully aware to what extent I had not ceased to be guided, and to what extent, now more visibly than ever, I am guided.

All the honors that have encouraged me, the distinctions, the proofs of friendship on the part of my colleagues, the signs of goodwill and solicitude on the part of my superiors, while they may be temporal things, have been testimony to the divine protection. I have lived by that, without on that account glorifying myself in words or boastings. All these signs of divine protection have sustained me and have enabled me to bear trials without bitterness and without rancor. The trials, then, have been banished as by a puff of wind. And all those signs of affection and honor have remained in my recollection as memories for which, in my religious life, I thank God, Who has heaped them upon me. As for the acts of renunciation I made before addressing myself to the proper quarter to seek entry into the religious life, especially when I offered my highest decorations to the Vicar of Jesus Christ, those acts corresponded to a compelling need to make manifest my gratitude toward God for all His goodness.

To say everything in a word: all my acts, all the stages of my temporal life and now also of my spiritual life, I have accomplished in spite of myself, with the sensible and visible assistance of the Most High. I have never known what the good God was preparing for me ... "What are Your plans, Lord? Show them to me. I have only to follow them."

I am a child, hardly knowing how to walk. I feel myself emboldened, and I am encouraged on all sides. I do not consider the circumstances; I advance. I advance; I advance without knowing it. I do not dare to advance, and nevertheless, through my whole life, I advance. There exists a picture showing the little Saint Thérèse called by the Child Jesus. At His call she runs to Him. That picture—that is my entire life. I am a child who is learning to walk; he does not dare to advance, but his mother makes a sign to him and, gazing toward her, he advances. The good God makes signs to me without ceasing, and I advance. The child advances toward his mother, and when, trembling, he comes into her arms, then he leaps, he laughs, he embraces her. That, when I shall come to God, will be my death.

## Postscript

As the original French edition of this work was appearing, in March 1945, there reached me a remarkable essay on *La Prière* ["Prayer"] (Plon, 1944). It came from the distinguished French physiologist Dr. Alexis Carrel, the author of *Man the Unknown*. I take from it some of his propositions:

Man is an indivisible whole.

To succeed, life must be led according to inflexible rules, which spring from its very structure. We run a grave risk when we allow some fundamental activity to die within us, whether it be of the physiological order, or of the intellectual, or of the spiritual.

Atrophy of the religious sense, and of the moral, shows itself to be as harmful as atrophy of the intelligence.

The religious sense is expressed above all in prayer.

It is by prayer that man goes to God ... "It is shameful to pray," wrote Nietzsche. In fact it is no more shameful

to pray than it is to drink or to breathe. Man needs God,
as he needs water and oxygen.

The best method of communion with God is, without
any doubt, the integral accomplishment of His will.

These propositions have the value of law. The consequences of their violation are more especially harmful
insofar as he who disregards them has a deeper and more
far-reaching social or political influence.

In connection with prayer, I am always surprised how
much, on the continent of Europe, people seem to be
unaware of the spiritual basis of the public life of President Roosevelt, as well as of his acts and declarations of a
religious character. I cite his taking the presidential oath
on the thirteenth chapter of the first Epistle of Saint Paul
to the Corinthians (the chapter deals with charity), and his
declarations on faith in God, on the practice of charity,
and on the Beatitudes.

I conclude this note with a saying of Lord Halifax, the
British minister for foreign affairs who declared war against
Nazi Germany: "Unless Europe is prepared to return to
Christian principles, it seems that we shall not be able
to make much progress in our relations, whether personal
or international" (House of Lords, April 19, 1939). That
applies to the whole world.

# THE CHRISTIAN VOCATION
# OF MY COUNTRY

*December 1943*

WE now have to touch upon a subject of a different character.

It is my task to give you an idea of the meeting of my country with the Catholic Church and of the vocation of the Benedictine monastic Order in the spiritual renewal of China. Finally, I shall have to consider my humble and exacting personal duty, as a man, as a patriot, and a diplomatist, as a Christian, as a monk and a priest, in the face of this fact, which is proclaimed with more clarity and more grandeur every day: the Christian vocation of China.

The designs of Providence are unfathomable.

The Roman Empire had extended its possessions even into that Asiatic land where the Messiah was born and where the Church was founded. If the Chinese Empire, which is much older, and which in the course of its history at one time extended even to the borders of Persia, had had some kind of protectorate in Palestine, the first disciples of Jesus might just as well, God wishing it so, have made their center at Beijing instead of at Rome, and the past two thousand years would have taken a totally different historical course. Let us not forget, however, that a thousand years pass as quickly as a single day in the sight of the Most High.

It was at the beginning of the Christian era that Buddhism penetrated into China.[1] Together with lofty and profound religious inspiration, it includes a medley of deadening superstitious beliefs, so that, if it has given spiritual comfort to many souls, it has never been in a position fully to draw them out of themselves or, *a fortiori*, to give sustenance to society, still less to the state.

What might have been the fortune of China and of the yellow race[2] if Christianity had been able at that time to come to us and to give the Confucianist moral and spiritual philosophy that higher light and that indestructible completion brought to humanity by Him Who possesses truly "the Words of eternal life"?

I could continue to raise such questions, through the whole length of history. They have their foundation in the unity of the human race, and they would bear witness to that profound harmony of Christianity with human nature and would bring out, in me, pain rather than sadness at the knowledge that the meeting of the Chinese people with Jesus Christ has always been postponed.

In the thirteenth century, in 1266, the emperor Kublai Khan, receiving at Beijing the father and the uncle of Marco Polo, charged them to go to the pope to ask him to send to China "a hundred doctors, wise in the seven arts". They would have built in China the imposing arches of the bridge between East and West.

Tell me, was there ever a sovereign who might have conceived so grandiose a plan for an embassy of peace? How far would Asia and Europe have been united and

---

[1] Buddhism arrived in China during the last half of the Han dynasty (202 B.C.–A.D. 220).—Ed.

[2] See p. 90, note 4.—Ed.

truly pacified if this brilliant group of Christian men of letters, distinguished, comprehensive, animated by faith, hope, and charity, had arrived in China, there to be the guests of the head of the state, invited, wanted, welcomed? The request remained without result.[3]

In every age, and even today, intellectuals are so much absorbed by their personal concern for the immediate work in which they are engaged that, among those thousands of men who give themselves to the study of the same disciplines, there are rarely a few dozen, or even a few individuals, who have the vision, the intellectual inspiration, to change their habits of mind, to enter into new horizons, to scale the mountain, or even to contemplate the other side of it.

In the seventeenth century—and this is the distinction of the Society of Jesus—a group of Jesuits, men of valor, of science, and of a lofty apostolic sense, who had arrived successively at Macao and had come into northern China, were summoned to Beijing.

Their talents, their disinterest, their courtesy quickly opened all doors to them, even to the doors of the Imperial Palace. You know the greatest names among them: Matteo Ricci, an Italian; Adam Schall, a German; Ferdinand Verbiest, a Belgian. They were appreciated; they were discussed. They were questioned about the secret reason for their coming and their activities. The integrity of their moral life was recognized, and many became interested in the religious faith that was the essential cause

---

[3] A Franciscan missionary group did travel to Beijing and founded a somewhat successful ministry in the late thirteenth and early fourteenth centuries. However, that mission was aimed at converting the Mongols who ruled China at the time rather than the Han Chinese people, so the spirit of Lu's critique is fair.—Ed.

of all their actions. They had given themselves wholly to the country of their evangelizing mission, and they had become Chinese subjects, being regarded as such by the court and by the emperor and treated as such to the point that public offices of a scientific character were conferred upon them, and even titles of nobility.

Father Matteo Ricci converted to the Catholic religion the Minister of State Xu Guangqi and gave to him in baptism the Christian name of Paul, indicating by this choice the high vocation that he desired for him.

Paul Xu responded admirably to the graces that Heaven bestowed upon him. He was the head and the heart of a group of high-minded Christians and remarkable *literati*, among whom must be cited in particular Michael Yang Qiyuan and Leo Li Wocun, whose exceptional work has survived to this day and retains an authority and fame that will not cease to grow.[4] Matteo Ricci, Adam Schall, Ferdinand Verbiest, and their brethren, and with them Paul Xu, Michael Yang, Leo Li, and their colleagues, laid the first foundations of the Catholic Church in China; foundations on which, alas, the emissaries of the Church have for three centuries found it very difficult to continue to build the edifice so magnificently begun.

I should like to pass very rapidly over that sad and arduous period that stretches from the quarrel of the Europeans over the Rites down to the contemporary renewal; a period that the great Popes Benedict XV, Pius XI, and His Holiness Pius XII have earned the singular distinction of bringing to an end. A quarter of a century has been enough

---

[4] The two figures Lu is referring to here are more typically identified as Yang Tingyun 楊廷筠 and Li Zhizao 李之藻 in contemporary literature (Lu uses other, still accurate name conventions for them). Together, Xu, Yang, and Li are considered the Three Pillars of Chinese Catholicism.—Ed.

for them to reach one of the greatest turning points in the spiritual history of mankind.

I will sum up the whole of this epoch by saying that it was a time of misunderstandings and, in consequence, of mistrust. And when in the nineteenth century the Catholic missions, which had become wholly extinct, again began to make progress, their labors were obstructed in our country for a second reason, by a state of confusion that, again, it will suffice to recall as briefly as possible.

I have already described to you the extent to which the weakness of the last decades of the Chinese Empire had drawn upon us the greed of foreigners and how difficult it had been for the newborn republic to restore the international situation of my country. The fact that those spreading the Gospel were subjects of these foreign powers alone made their task from the first extremely delicate, and very little was needed for them to be regarded by public opinion as the advance-guards of a foreign domination. And alas, some regrettable events brought about most sad confusions in this matter. It happened thus that by force of circumstances the Church became, in the eyes of the Chinese, the scapegoat for most of the political injustices of which my country was the object and nearly the victim. I will confine myself here to recalling, among a thousand others, one only of those unhappily important events, which I have personally a right to cite because it came about in opposition to a decision of the government in which I had the honor to have taken the initiative.

From my first entry into the government, convinced of the higher importance of spiritual values and of the support they bring to the nations that hold them in honor, I dreamed of obtaining for the Chinese state the spiritual cooperation of the Catholic Church, whose work and life I had studied for many years and of which I had become a member. An opportunity for this being presented, with the agreement of the Council of Ministers, I begged the vicar-apostolic of Beijing to have the goodness to sing an official *Te Deum*, to bring upon the Chinese state the blessing of the Most High. This ceremony was an innovation for which there was no precedent. It took place in the Bei Tang church.[5] The diplomatic corps was present. The purpose was to introduce publicly a new spirit into the relations of the Chinese state with the religion of Jesus Christ and with the Catholic Church. And in my mind, this act was only a first beginning.

In fact, in 1917, I had the opportunity to go much farther. I proposed to the government that we should come to an understanding with the Holy See about the establishment of diplomatic relations between the republic and the papal court. This proposal having been accepted, I put myself in touch with the Vatican, which soon indicated its agreement. The intervention and the absolute and systematic opposition of the government of a great European power[6] that declared that it was concerned to "protect" the missions obliged us to abandon this project, so simple and so straightforward, which had to wait more than a quarter of a century, until February 1943, before it could be carried out. How could it be otherwise, in these circumstances, than that the public opinion of a non-Christian country should indeed be led into error about the Catholic missions, about the Church, and about Christianity itself?

From the historical point of view, this unhappy question, and all those connected with it, are perhaps inexhaustible.

---

[5] Lit., "the North Church", referring to the Church of the Savior in Beijing, one of the most historic and significant Roman Catholic churches in China.—Ed.

[6] I.e., France.—Ed.

But to draw advantage from the lessons of history, it is necessary to know both how to learn and how to forget. . . .
I have said enough about this. It is not the past that must have our attention; it is the future.

The sacrifices endured by the little band of Chinese Christians, and its numerous martyrs, who had the heroism to bear, to the very end, the painful consequences of all these misunderstandings; the sacrifices, sometimes carried even to death, of many missionaries, the victims of circumstances, seeing no way out of the difficulties surrounding them; the pastoral loyalty with which, and, in the most recent example, in the course of the present war, the Catholic missionaries have remained in the midst of our people through all dangers and have helped and encouraged them, verily showing once again how greatly they love them; the sacrifices and the blood so lavishly spilt, today and for so many years, by the Chinese people for the defense of their national independence, of their moral dignity, and of their territorial integrity—all these holocausts speak for us before God, very much better than we could ourselves.

To put an end to a situation so confused and to enlighten the unfavorable public opinion that it had inevitably created, words were no longer of any use. Only deeds could correct, little by little, so entangled a situation. They can do so all the better since—and this is a basic element in our national character—the Chinese people, when they are opposed to a given attitude, are not at all disposed blindly to adopt an opposite attitude, liking, on the contrary, to keep the balance of the golden mean, happy to give proof of a moral greatness and a large-mindedness that the most distinguished personalities of our nation have always cultivated.

You are familiar with the outline of the first years of the renewal of the Catholic apostolate in China. The movement's pioneer was that dear hero of our faith, the son of a Belgian father and an English mother, Fr. Vincent Lebbe, who has left in Belgium and France the deep marks of his apostolic vision and his courageous zeal. He was the soldier of the papacy in China, always in the front line, obedient, humble, ascetic, tireless, persecuted without cease and without cease forgetting yesterday's ordeals so as to embrace the apostolic duty of the present hour with freedom of spirit and to carry it out without faltering to the very end.

Following the example of Ricci, of Schall, and of Verbiest, so as to give himself wholly to the country to which he burned to give the Gospel, Fr. Lebbe, in his turn, sought to become a Chinese citizen.[7] He asked for and obtained naturalization. I emphasize this fact, for it is relevant and of very great importance. And I am still more happy to emphasize it since Providence has called me to become a monk in an abbey whose founder, charged by the Holy Father with a monastic and apostolic work in Brazil, took a similar step. Even before he had laid the first stone of this house, Msgr. Gérard van Calden became, from 1896—and these are his own words—"a Brazilian by affection and by naturalization".

Such instances are not only gestures. They are the expressions of a profound attitude of mind. They affirm a manner of seeing, of judging and acting, in the exercise of which the missionary incorporates himself into the nation

---

[7] Lebbe, originally a Vincentian missionary, was renowned for his defense of Chinese interests and his stance against imperial aggression from the French and became a Chinese citizen in 1928. For an account of his story, see Jacques Leclerq, *Thunder in the Distance: The Life of Père Lebbe*, trans. George Lamb (New York: Sheed and Ward, 1958).—Ed.

of which he becomes at once the apostle and the son. In this respect, they are precedents that the example, the precepts, and the deeds of the Apostle Saint Paul and all the tradition of the primitive Church support and justify with an inalienable authority.

The most comprehensive document of the apostolic movement begun by Fr. Lebbe is, I think, the letter that, in 1917, he wrote to the vicar-apostolic of Ningbo. It was addressed to the Holy See, and it gives a striking picture of the religious situation, the remedying of which the popes themselves were about to direct.

In 1919, Benedict XV published the encyclical *Maximum Illud*, and in 1922 he set up an apostolic delegation in China, the first incumbent of which, Msgr. Costantini,[8] in execution of the papal wishes, opened the way to a great revival.

Seven years later, Pius XI took up again and developed in the encyclical *Rerum Ecclesia* the whole program of his predecessor; then he himself consecrated, in Saint Peter's, Rome, the first Chinese bishops;[9] and veritably seized every opportunity to express by word and by deed a solicitude ever on the alert and a wish to tackle, in order to solve, the whole problem of the relations between the Far East and Christianity. In 1928, he expressed forcibly his "full confidence that the legitimate

[8] Celso Benigno Luigi Costantini, made cardinal in 1953, served as missionary in China from 1922 to 1933 and was a significant figure in transitioning the Chinese Catholic churches from foreign missionary governance to native Chinese leadership. He served in the Congregation for the Propagation of the Faith from 1935 to 1953.—Ed.

[9] Historically, the first native Chinese named bishop was Gregory Luo Wenzao (1616–1691), consecrated in 1685. However, there were no other native Chinese bishops until 1926, when Pius XI consecrated six bishops. Today they are called the first modern Chinese bishops.—Ed.

aspirations and the rights of a nation numerically the greatest on earth, a nation of ancient culture that has known greatness and splendors, will be fully recognized"; adding that, if the Chinese nation "knows how to keep itself in the paths of justice and order, she will not fail to enter a great future."

Pius XI died, leaving to him who was to succeed him the continuation of a task in which the latter had been his immediate collaborator.

His Holiness Pius XII, from the outset of his pontificate, resolved the question of the Rites, overcoming the primordial obstacle that held the Catholic Church and Chinese society apart from one another.[10] Three years later, he received the letters of credence of the first minister plenipotentiary of China to be accredited to the papal court.

The creation of a Chinese legation at the Vatican bears witness to a considerable moral victory of China and of the Holy See. It emphasizes the agreement of the social doctrines of the Chinese state with those of the Church, and it accompanies the growth in the number of Chinese Catholics, whose annual increase in five years (from 1931 to 1936; there do not yet exist, I believe, more recent general statistics) has risen by a hundred percent.

A new era has plainly opened. It would be considerably to reduce its grandeur not to acknowledge fully the immense program that God reserves for it.

I could not better describe the way this apostolic revival will follow than in recalling the clear and courageous

---

[10] Pius XII directed the Congregation for the Propagation of the Faith to issue the instruction *Plane compertum* in 1939, which relaxed many of the previous restrictions placed on Chinese Catholics in the early eighteenth century.—Ed.

terms in which Msgr. Costantini defines its new point of departure. I find them in the masterly essay he dedicated to the memory of Msgr. François Pallu, the founder of the Paris Foreign Missions, which was published in the *Osservatore Romano* of January 25, 1940. These few brief quotations take a character that seems virtually decisive from their intrinsic clarity and from the authority given them by the apostolic career of their author and by the important positions with which he is entrusted. The secretary of the Sacred Congregation for the Propagation of the Faith expresses himself thus:

> The missions, by themselves, are not the Church; they are a preparation for the foundation of the Church." "We have founded in the Far East, not the Church, with her normal organization, but the foreign missions; and Asia has not been converted." "The apostles and the missionaries of the sub-apostolic age founded the Church with local clergy, and they converted the Western world.
>
> What was the method used by the missionaries of the apostolic and post-apostolic age? Do we use the same methods?
>
> We use entirely different methods, which seem to us more perfect, but which the experience of four centuries has shown to be practically sterile.
>
> The missionaries of those first ages built up the Church with the native hierarchy of the country, and they used for the liturgy the language they found on the spot.... We have attempted to convert the East through a foreign hierarchy and through Latin, and the East has not responded.
>
> In 1615, Pope Paul V, in compliance with the wishes of Saint Robert Bellarmine, had accorded to China the use of the Chinese literary language for the liturgy, which would have followed the Latin rite. The concession was not implemented.

This aspect of the problem also did not escape Msgr. Pallu, and he eagerly waited until, in 1673, the privilege previously conceded to the Jesuits was accorded to him.

How many missionaries have poured out their lives in these regions of ancient civilization, preaching the Gospel there! They form an immense army; and sanctity, zeal, science, and the favor of the political powers have not been lacking among them. But what are the results? *Et erat videre miseriam* (and it was to see misery).

For the whole of Asia,

> We count hardly nine millions of Christians out of a thousand million pagans. If in the Far East the Catholic Church is increasing annually by 200,000 Christians, the number of pagans and of Mahometans is increasing, through the birthrate, by at least ten millions.
>
> When will the problem be solved?

The conclusion is evident:

> Go back, in missionary work, to apostolic methods: *Riportare le Missioni ai metodi apostolici.*

I should like to be allowed to add certain considerations to this account of the very great problem presented to Christianity by the fact of the gigantic civilizations of Asia and, in particular, by the civilization of the Far East.

The civilization of the Far East is that of a people whose history as a nation goes back four thousand years and who alone represent half the population of Asia and a quarter of mankind: 450 million men and women, of the same race and the same spirit, among whom, as is the case with the whole of the population of Asia, there is not a certain one percent that is Christian, whether Catholic or Protestant.

The language of this people is by itself the language of a third of mankind: a linguistic fact unique in the world and without any possible comparison.

In its terms and its expressions, the Chinese literary language has an exceptional conciseness and precision. Its deep beauty, its vigor, and its elegance have for thousands of years been the abiding and noble treasure of the Far East.

Now, between the Chinese language and those that use alphabets, there is a difference of conception that is complete.[11] In Chinese, a man writes what the eye sees; in the languages that use alphabets, a man writes what the mouth pronounces.

In order to pass from the one to the others, or *vice versa*, he must accept the labor of a new education, at once linguistic and literary. Only a limited number of men are capable of it.

Insofar as among us—at least in her singing and in the prayers and readings that priests and people recite aloud— the Catholic liturgy will have been unable to adopt the Chinese literary language (which, as I like to insist, is admirably suited to the Gregorian chant), to that extent the worship that the Church renders to God—the sacrifice of the Mass, the Divine Office, the liturgy of the sacraments, the admirable Catholic liturgy of the dead—will remain an absolutely closed book for the yellow race.[12] The people of the Far East cannot become acquainted with it; they

---

[11] Lu is here referring to the system of ideographs used in Chinese writing, across all Chinese dialects. Today, there are ways of representing the sounds ideographs represent using alphabetic script, but there is no native alphabetic script in Chinese. This is distinctive of the Chinese language, as both Korean and Japanese developed alphabetic representations to either supplement or displace ideographs.—Ed.

[12] The use of vernacular languages rather than ecclesial Latin for Mass became standard after liturgical reforms following the promulgation of *Sacrosanctum Concilium* in 1963, as part of Vatican II, fifteen years after Lu's book was published in English.—Ed.

cannot, therefore, feel the need of it or conceive a desire for it; and, in consequence, they have no normal means of taking any advantage of it whatsoever. In default of that measure of adaptation which I believe to be the prerequisite of all important apostolic action, in five hundred or a thousand years evangelizing efforts will not have modified in any considerable fashion the very small proportion represented by the number of Christians and of Catholics in a population that will itself have increased beyond its present numbers in proportions that it is vain to seek to forecast.

The proposal to adopt a new language in the liturgy in the Far East may arouse in some excellent minds the fear of separating the Church in China from the rest of the Church in a way that would deprive Far Eastern Christianity of certain higher benefits with which the course of history has enriched the Universal Church. Greek and Latin patristic literature is an incomparable treasure. Catholic theology borrowed from Greece the philosophical foundations of her spiritual edifice, and the terrestrial government of the Church found in Rome the juridical concepts that form the framework of her hierarchy and of her admirable organization. Moreover, the contemporary intellectual movement among ecclesiastics is developing to a great extent in Latin. All these good things have a value that is inestimable. In wishing to give the Chinese population access to the practice of the Catholic religion, it is not necessary to limit the participation of our clergy in the heritage of two thousand years of the life of the Church or to place obstacles in the way of the fraternal relations of the Church in China with the episcopate and clergy of all the Universal Church.

That is as clear as can be.

So, at a time when we are waiting and hoping for the introduction of the Chinese language in the liturgy, it is important that our clergy, far from diminishing their studies in Greco-Latin culture, shall develop them still more, in such a way that the Church in China assimilates and possesses fully those ancient and actual good things that are traditionally Catholic and Roman and which, far from being in any way incompatible with our ancestral character, will be, in our country too, in the members of the Catholic clergy, a splendid ornament and a noble enrichment.

Under these conditions, the introduction of the Chinese literary language into the Catholic liturgy could not lead to any undesirable consequence and appears as the leading feature of that revival of apostolic methods that calls with such insistence for our prayer and meditation, our study and our action.

But I should like to go several stages farther along this way.

To make reasonable progress, the revival of which I have sketched one aspect, cannot, it seems to me, remain unilateral. The cultural ties that bind the peoples of a Greco-Latin intellectual formation to the Church of Rome are a human foundation for the maintenance and the development of the Catholic religion in the Western countries, which are all to a large extent the heirs of ancient Greece and ancient Rome. It seems, then, indispensable to forge also cultural links, as strong as possible, between the capital of universal Christianity and the yellow race.

While, on the one hand, the Chinese clergy will preserve and develop their acquaintance with Greco-Latin culture earnestly and intelligently, it would, on the other hand, be unutterably precious—and how such a step would be appreciated by my entire country!—it would, I say, be unutterably precious if the pontifical clergy in Rome could include among its members and its personalities some body of distinguished men who, in the very center of Catholicism, would have carried out the opposite process, having acquired and possessing one or another of the great non-European cultures of the world, beginning with that which is the most important of them all, since it includes a third part of mankind.

The work and the effort that this second part of the program would demand should not appear excessive. Many gifted young men are in a position to undertake it. To succeed in it, it is only necessary that they apply themselves to it.

The results of this work would infinitely exceed the trouble it would require. It would enable the Mother Church of all the churches not only to be the spiritual capital of the Christian world but to become the cultural and moral capital of the entire globe.

This twofold cultural movement in the Church—in China Sino-Latin, in Rome Latino-Chinese—would be one of the most noble and the most splendid human manifestations of the unity of spirit and of heart in the Church of Christ. It would give a natural, normal, and solid foundation to the propagation of the Catholic Faith in the Far East, and, from there, throughout Asia, through which the grace of God would very abundantly perform its supernatural work.

It is a sign of the times, it is the sign of a great spiritual victory of the Church, that one should be able openly to dilate upon a problem of this magnitude at this opportune moment; a problem that has remained without correction and without solution through so many centuries. In raising it in the columns of the *Osservatore Romano*, Msgr. Costantini has once again deserved well of the Church and of mankind.

And now I reach the second subject of this last section of my book. What are the vocation and the function of

Benedictine monasticism in developing the foundation of the Church in China?

Contrary to what my compatriots thought when they learned of my entry into the cloister, a Benedictine monastery is not a tomb. It is not even a hermitage. It is a family, a *familia*, and one of the most ancient and most characteristic institutions of that great family of God that is called the Catholic Church. For this reason, it is particularly well qualified to give the hierarchy and diocesan clergy of China, and at the same time Chinese society, an active, *familiar*, and religious assistance, a fraternal support, which will only be complete when Benedictine monasticism has gained within my country sufficient suitable recruits for the spirit of Saint Benedict to take root among the élite of our best minds and our greatest hearts.

I should like to invite my compatriots to make a brief stay in the guesthouse of the Abbey of Saint Andrew, and I should like to say to them: "Read the Rule of Saint Benedict, observe the family life we lead, see how we conceive and organize prayer and work, and study how we Chinese might be able to adopt that Rule, which is a synthesis of Christianity, and to introduce it and to apply it among our people." I would add: "At present Chinese monasticism is Buddhist. What would our country be today if that monasticism had been Benedictine?"

Not being able profitably to extend such an invitation, I have sent to as many of my friends as I have been able copies of the Rule of Saint Benedict, in Chinese, in English, and in French. I have been greatly encouraged by the attentiveness with which they have acquainted themselves with it and by the impressions of it that they have communicated to me. On the occasion of my ordination to the priesthood, they gave an exceptional distinction to the expressions of their sympathy and affection, which was, on their part and on the part of the government of the republic, an unaccustomed tribute to the Catholic priesthood, to Holy Church, and, at the same time, to the Rule of Saint Benedict.

You will permit me to quote a brief extract from one of these tributes, which I have already, in other circumstances, quoted at greater length. It comes from a group of twenty high personalities of my country. I should like you to forget that it mentions my name and to consider only the principles to which it relates:

> Mr. Lu knows the Chinese moral philosophy, and now he becomes a priest in the West. He absorbs, then, in the West, the best that the West possesses.... He works to discover what there is in common between the two hemispheres and, eventually, to complete it. He will realize in himself the fusion of East and West in the moral sphere. He will show that in the West, just as in China, material civilization does not have precedence over spiritual civilization. And thereby he will work also to further justice and peace in his country....
>
> We do not think that European civilization is solely utilitarian ... Mr. Lu,... makes a comparison between the Chinese and European civilizations ... and it is not only on your old friends that you will confer a favor. The whole of China will benefit from what you give us.

Those words are an attractive and pressing invitation. How could I resist that appeal, which corresponds to my former anticipations, to my convictions of today, and to my most cherished desire? Those words are an appeal to the whole of Benedictine monasticism, and I would have failed in my duty if I had not reported them here. My friends have not seen what I have seen and what I have confirmed for more than sixteen years, but they anticipate very clearly the fruits of peace and of life that the cooperation between East and West desired by them cannot fail to bring. Their sentiment bears out the very precise program that, so many times, the first apostolic delegate in China never ceased to indicate to the Benedictines, to whom he suggested a work in the Far East of which the grandeur is not less than that of the Rule of Saint Benedict itself; that is: "To conserve and deepen the ancient national culture of China, in giving it the rejuvenation of Christianity." What greater program for monastic and apostolic work than that!

The Benedictines have up to the present hardly touched the Far East.

At the time of my entry into the Abbey of Saint Andrew, that monastery had lately undertaken the foundation of a priory in the province of Sichuan. The most unexpected circumstances suddenly brought the capital of China to the region where that modest cloister is situated when it was transported provisionally to Chongqing and permitted the priory, through the agency of three of its members, to give modest but very eager assistance to our country in her danger. It was then that I believed that the moment had come for me to offer an English copy of the Rule of Saint Benedict in homage to the First Lady of China. In the very kind letter in which Madame Chiang Kai-Shek was good enough to thank me, she writes these few words, which demonstrate once again the true moral and spiritual harmony between East and West: "I have read the Rule of Saint Benedict with a profound admiration. What a noble way of life; and at the same time, how wise and simple! I have been very much impressed by this book."

It is a great comfort to me to be able to quote that declaration. I like to conclude from it that the Rule of Saint Benedict will not fail, in the hour chosen by Providence, to be understood by the East, to be admired and loved among our people, and to be practiced by them.

I should like here to address myself to the Benedictine monks, of whatever country, who will do me the honor of reading these pages.

In the seventh century of the Christian era, a Chinese Buddhist monk, wishing to give true monasticism to his country, left for the West and lived for seventeen years in the monasteries of India, fully acquainting himself with their doctrines and traditions, their observances and the whole of their life. After that he returned to China, assisting powerfully in giving to Buddhist monasticism an impulse that, having become irresistible, was to bring about the spread of Buddhism into all the provinces of the whole country. This monk was called Xuanzang.

You may be assured that I have meditated long on the vocation of Xuanzang; and today I cannot refrain from telling you the question that many are asking themselves about us in my country: "Is Benedictine monasticism inferior or superior to Buddhist monasticism?"

One thing is certain, and that is that Buddhist monasticism in China has been the great instrument of the spread of Buddhism through the entire country. Is Benedictine monasticism in a position to take part on the same scale in spreading and establishing Christianity through the whole of China—to take a part of which the apostolic result would be incalculable?

Many times have my friends expressed to me their regret that the dear priory founded by Saint Andrew's in the Province of Sichuan should be still somewhat isolated, and they have asked me when my brethren in China will have the very great joy of being no longer all alone among us. You will know how much I share that sentiment. May we not, then, pray God that the whole Benedictine Order may consider and come to understand this vast problem and that, in a great movement of monastic expansion and of charity, it may set about doubling the number of its own houses by as many new foundations, wisely and courageously undertaken, from Mukden[13] to Canton, from the Pacific coasts even to the high mountains of Central Asia?

I am not worthy to be a Benedictine Xuanzang, but perhaps, during my lifetime or after my death, the Lord will cause His own glory to shine so much the more because, among so many millions of Chinese, to help in bringing the Rule of Saint Benedict to China, He has been willing to recruit one weak old man.

[13] I.e., Shenyang, China.—Ed.

# CONCLUSION

T HIS account, at once too long and too short, of the divine favors that have accompanied me from the cradle to old age, and of those also with which Providence, I have no doubt, will endow my country, demands a conclusion filled with filial trust in the Lord.

The soul of man is immortal. The body grows old and requires care and attention. The spirit, too, may grow old or may mature; but inasmuch as it matures, it bears fruit, and its richness brings a contentment that, believe me, offers more attraction than all the charms of a smiling and ardent youth. The serenity of the old in itself bears witness that the human soul is spiritual and that it is immortal.

Heaven ordained that I should be a man of the old China, having bent my back under the heavy authority of the imperial officials, with their stereotyped usages and customs and their habitually insolent attitude; an attitude all the more insolent since they knew themselves to be hardly allowed to kiss the ground before the emperor, at any rate if the greatest favor conceded to them was not limited to being allowed to gaze upon the walls of the palace from outside.

Heaven ordained also that, from my childhood, I should have a keen awareness of the demands of human dignity and of the sacrifices that the honor of being a man require. I was, then, for a very long time, a hidden revolutionary, without prejudices and without bitterness, taking my inspiration from ancient and unchanging principles and wishing for a public life that might conform to those principles. Those principles can animate various forms of government. A good government requires of the statesmen that their intelligence, their experience, and their disinterest enable them to be both clearsighted and farsighted. One single man of great importance can make the happiness or unhappiness of a nation. The nation is always led to imitate those who govern it. When the state is in equilibrium, the nation cannot fail to be happy.

Heaven desired that I should meet, in the first stages of my public career, an eminent master who was to give his life in witness to his principles. When, on July 29, 1900, Mr. Xu Jingcheng was, with three other political personalities, led toward the infamous scaffold destined for them, one of the condemned, furious at the ignominy of which he was the object, turned toward the representative of the minister of justice and exclaimed to him: "Today it is for me—tomorrow it is for you!" Mr. Xu Jingcheng, taking his companion in misfortune gently by the sleeve, said to him simply: "This is not the time to speak; let us be silent." It was with that last act of dignity and charity that he committed his spirit.

Could I dare to envy such a death, suffered by such a master?

Now it was that Heaven caused me, under the influence of this dear master, to shift my ground, I might say, from the Old Testament to the New, from a vague and confused Christian mentality to the knowledge of the full truth, from the hope of salvation to salvation itself. I became a member of the Catholic and Apostolic Church, the Roman Church; I became a monk, and I became a priest. What a revolution! And how much I wish that the spiritual life—which, in the last resort, is the sole true strength enabling man to be fully man—how much I wish that the spiritual life of my people and that of the whole world might be enlightened by that light toward which Minister Xu Jingcheng showed me the way.

We diplomatists cannot be egoists, and we have to bear in mind that the happiness of our peoples, for each of us, is bound up with the happiness of the neighboring peoples and with that of the entire world. How wisely does Confucianism teach when it gives the statesman for his highest task the pacification of the world.

We Catholic priests do not wish to and cannot place ourselves above the ministers of any other religion, but we wish—with Jesus Christ, with the Virgin Mary who remains standing at the foot of the Cross while her Son, insulted and mocked, dies there—we wish only to sacrifice ourselves that our people and all peoples may enter into a clear understanding of the spiritual kingdom of peace and of holiness to which God calls all men, to give them all the gift of happiness on earth, by the knowledge and the practice of that spiritual life whose blessedness death consecrates and makes eternal.

Europe—can I say it?—has known so little of the true wealth that was showered upon it from century to century by so many saints—and in what abundance! So many Europeans know Jesus Christ so little or are quite unaware of Him "Who is come into this world and Whom *His own* have not received". So many European statesmen are completely in error about that unique spiritual power which is wielded by the vicar of Jesus Christ, the pope Many of them have not taken the trouble to observe objectively and to study with attention the government and the work of the Holy See and the Church. They are unaware of the effective significance and importance of the pontifical acts, and when they read certain of those acts, is it not, perhaps, superficially? They do not see the immense benefit that every country is in a position to derive from the effective participation of the Holy See in the spiritual life of mankind.

And in China, how many men are there who, desiring to put into practice the maxims of the founder of the republic,[1] have never asked themselves questions about the worldwide spiritual strength of Catholicism and of Christianity and have not drawn from evidence so easy to obtain the conclusions that are imposed? They have not said to themselves that, if it is necessary, according to the testament of Dr. Sun Yat-sen, to "associate ourselves with those peoples who, in the common struggle, treat us on a basis of equality", the Catholic Church, which numbers three hundred and fifty million of the faithful, and her government, whose moral influence extends far beyond the seven hundred million Christians, act and wish to act toward us "not only on the basis of a perfect equality but with a feeling of true and most especial sympathy": that is the phrase of Pope Pius XI, on the morrow of our national unification, on August 1, 1928. They have not seen clearly that this gigantic spiritual organism might be for the Chinese people, the people of Confucius and of Dr. Sun Yat-sen, a most precious ally whose cooperation will give us, for the spiritual renovation of the heritage of our ancestors and for its intellectual and moral diffusion abroad, a support whose profound efficacy will greatly surpass the expectations of the most optimistic.

That is not at all to suggest that the pope might have to interfere in the political government of men, which belongs to the civil authority; still less to suggest that in the

[1] A reference to Sun Yat-sen.—Ed.

religious field pressure might be brought to bear on the conscience or the independence of anyone, for the religious act must of its essence be made freely. But it is to bring about, between the Holy See and the governments, a work of mutual information on the moral needs and the spiritual aspirations of men, a sincere respect for their various situations and various conditions, and a disposition for good understanding. It is to bring about also a desire in various quarters to be freed from certain habits of mind that in the long run form among upright and intelligent men an inferiority complex, arising out of the fact that they have themselves been able to change standards that ought to be fixed.

These words are far from being a reproach; they are an expression of devotion and attachment and good wishes.

Since I have spoken of Europe, I cannot omit to express here my affectionate gratitude to this dear country of Belgium, to which I owe my life's companion and in which I have received, through long and precious years, a Christian and religious hospitality that is a source of great happiness to me; in which, also, I see before my eyes the social advantages of a sincere understanding of the state with the Church, bringing about, between those two societies, a cooperation particularly effective for the good of society, of the family, and of the individual. During this Second World War, the Belgian people has again proved itself great in spirit. The union of all the spiritual forces of the nation has triumphed over the enemy, and the nation has found in the hierarchy of the Church as strong a support as that which she received during the last war. The world's turmoil has strengthened in Belgium the solidarity of all in the service of justice and of peace, under the silent aegis of the prisoner-king, the first citizen of his country, who, in the heroic love he bears for his people, has become, under an avalanche of misfortune, the Father of the Nation.

I dare to hope, for our peoples as for myself, for the light and the joy of Christianity.

If I have been able by the grace of God to embrace the monastic life with so much joy and to rise to the priesthood, I have confidence that this will not be to call from Heaven blessings empty of sense and meaning, but, by virtue of the merits of my Master and Lord Jesus Christ, the Master of masters, the Lord of lords, to give to all those whom I love, and they are innumerable, the desire to know God still more, to be borne toward Him, and to be, not His slaves, but His children.

Therefore, my dear countrymen—for I cannot but give you the last of the thoughts I here express—therefore, believe in my affection and my experience: our families will be happy; our young people, or at least their great *élite*, will receive the strength to overcome themselves and to progress, in work, in moral stature, and in joy; our populations will live in security and, gradually, in plenty; and the whole of China will be regarded among the nations as a gentle and a strong people, knowing how, if it is necessary, to bring to their senses those who love war, courteous toward all, and recognizing the courtesies done to it, loving others, loved by others, and blessed by God.

May God, in all the nations of the earth, be honored and glorified!

# LETTER TO MY FRIENDS IN GREAT BRITAIN AND AMERICA

SOME of my English friends, having read the original edition of my *Souvenirs et Pensées*, asked me to develop the pages of that book which deal with the character of my country, with the relations between Chinese civilization and Christian civilization, with the relations that the Chinese nation and people already have with the Christian and Catholic Church.

I am touched by the sympathy that inspires this request, but I fear the responsibility I am asked to undertake. Is it possible to establish in summary form so vast a synthesis as that expected of me? Is not to attempt it to run the risk of bewildering rather than enlightening the reader?

The pages of *Souvenirs et Pensées* are barely an outline. To meet the wishes expressed to me, it seems to me that I should have to transform that outline into a great fresco, a sort of Last Judgment wherein would figure the whole of China, all the Orient, and, in consequence, all the Occident.

I am not a worker of miracles, and I feel myself unequal to such an undertaking.

I am obliged, then, to disappoint this kind expectation and to confine myself to adding a second outline to the first. Undoubtedly it is as imperfect as the former. But if it can supply any new knowledge to my friends of the West, it is my desire that, far from satisfying their desires, it may stimulate them and lead them to approach the Confucianist world and the Chinese world more closely and by their own researches.

# I

White men and yellow men, we who have been meeting each other for some hundreds of years, we have considered too little that our two races are both of them human; we have too seldom asked ourselves about the deep psychological and moral kinship existing between the ancient and always living civilization of the Far East and the Christian civilization that, long prepared among the Hebrews, has found its principal manifestations among the various peoples springing from Europe and America.

We have accentuated a natural tendency to find our satisfaction in the possession of our own endowments. This self-sufficiency has led the Chinese to shut themselves in upon themselves, and Europeans to regard contemptuously those who are strangers to them.

Today Providence is taking it upon itself to overcome the distances of a material order that separate us. It invites us to travel along the cultural and spiritual roads that run between us.

A number of those roads have already been charted. It is enough to set out upon them, and they will of themselves become broader.

We advance each to encounter the other. When we have met and understood, we shall feel keen regret not to have been known to one another very much sooner.

I invite my readers to accompany me along one of the roads that cross the frontiers between yellow men and white. To introduce them to this region, I have recourse to a very distinguished Englishman, the late Mr. Laurence Binyon. At home in the world of art and beauty, he is one of those Europeans who have best understood some of the profound aspects of the civilization of the Far East.

Mr. Binyon starts from a high point of departure: the art and philosophy of the Greeks, the qualities of purity and depth in the heritage that the Greeks bequeathed to the West. He observes:

> The average man is hardly aware at all of the enormous debt he owes to that rich past, the fruits of which he uses and enjoys; that deep-rooted tradition of life and thought which stands so majestic in its continuity through all the turmoil of Western history.

And he continues:

> That ancient civilization of which we are the heirs is indeed a magnificent achievement of human reason. But it is not, as it has seemed for so many centuries, the only measure and standard by which we may judge of civilization. We can no longer inhabit it as a closed garden of the mind, believing that nothing outside it really matters. Our horizons have widened; the far has been brought near. And I feel that in the future when we speak of "the humanities" we shall have to incorporate in that conception not only the legacy of the Mediterranean world, but the contribution of Asia to the art and thought of mankind.[1]

But unhappily the most distinguished, the most receptive of Europeans, even while admiring "the gorgeous East", have "found in those far countries no lodge for mind or spirit. And even today, for most of us in the West, the continent of Asia remains picturesque and exotic and awakens no response in the world of thought."[2]

---

[1] *The Spirit of Man in Asian Art*, by Laurence Binyon (Cambridge, Mass.: Harvard University Press, 1935), 8.

[2] Ibid., 12.

Such is the strength, the tenacity of the classical tradition, that the French nation has cherished perhaps more exclusively than any other. But there is one other country in the world that has formed and fostered a tradition of art and life even more powerful and persistent, and in the end even more exclusive; and that is China. Everywhere in Asia it is the art of China that, like Greek art in Europe, has enjoyed the greatest prestige. And the Chinese, at any rate since the Middle Ages, have tended to regard, and still regard, other nations, just as did the Greeks, as barbarians.

And the author concludes: "Let us turn, then, to China."[3]

I will add: let us cease to be each "barbarians" for the other. Let us no longer take our information solely from those among us who, chronologically, have been the first to encounter, to "discover", and to judge populations and races different to our own—that is to say, the traders, whose interest is limited to supply and demand; the soldiers, with whom contact is not always made without injury; the politicians, often dominated by the single thought of absorbing, for the profit of their country, the wealth of the peoples who are materially weakest; and, finally, all those, even though they be missionaries, who by a deplorable deficiency have been subject to the influence of misunderstandings that these various categories of men preoccupied with their own affairs have taken no trouble to dispel.

Let us see for ourselves, with the wholehearted desire to be fully men and to conduct ourselves as men, before God and toward the rest of mankind, what it is that is lacking in our respective "humanities" ...

The Chinese have possessed a veritable wealth in their moral and cultural treasure, and that wealth, which represents the genius of the Far East, has been enough for them.

[3] Ibid., 13.

Contrary to all the civilizations and all the languages that were their contemporaries in antiquity and that are today "dead" languages and extinct civilizations, museum-pieces piously preserved by more or less distant heirs, the Chinese language and civilization still live, as the Chinese people still live—the Chinese who, up to quite recent times, like the Western world itself, sincerely believed that they alone represented the human race. They are, moreover, a quarter or a third of that race.

What is the fundamental principle, the "precious pearl", of human life in the Far East?

I have on several occasions drawn the attention of my readers to the intellectual solicitude that is inherent in Confucianism and to the enquiries that it inspires.

To probe and to discover the problem of human life, to "possess" it, it is in the first place necessary, so a Confucianist believes, to acquire a personal and prolonged experience of the normal and profound functioning of that life. That experience can only be acquired in conforming one's self to all the requirements of life; that is to say, in obeying the Natural Law with perseverance of mind and heart and in not ceasing to advance in the perfection of this obedience.

This obedience is a condition, *sine qua non*, of all objective work. Inasmuch as we conform to the Natural Law does our personality develop its balance and its health and itself become a splendid terrain for our investigations of the laws of life, a laboratory well adapted to our study of man, of all that he is and of all that he can achieve.

This obedience demands a disciplined and constant effort, balanced and willing. If we should neglect it, if we should violate the Natural Law, might not our personality become deformed, so bringing about the distortion of our faculties of appreciation and judgment? How, in that event, could we truly know the being that we are?

The life of man is placed in that of his surroundings; that is to say, in the family. The life of the family is the social foundation on which all human existence, all the moral and spiritual progress of mankind, is built. This bedrock represents the principal object of the investigations dear to the thinkers of the Far East. Profound study of the life of man in his family surroundings reveals to us the manner in which society is formed and in which it is called to live. In the family we possess the pattern of the whole of society. The family is the soil whence we are sprung, whence our children are born and will be born, and in which is sown the seed of all the human race. How could we rate too highly the importance and the nobility of the fact of the family?

The fact of the family, as it is presented to us, the life of the family of which we are members, becomes, then, the object of our intellectual solicitude and of our constant observation. The value of our observation depends in the first place on the human level of our own family. It depends, next, on the balance and the depth of our judgments on it. If the life of our family is simple and large, human in the complete sense of that word, if we are able to observe it in an objective manner and to perceive it in its elements, what will not be our knowledge of man!

He who fully grasps what the life of the family is, he who lives that life fully, he indeed is a prince among mankind.

The bond of family life is filial piety. It is the fruit of the indissoluble affection that parents bring to each other and of that which they together bring to their children. Through that bond the family attains its perfection.

Filial piety gives to man the consciousness of his *filiation*, of what he receives at his entry into life, of what life is for him who receives it, and whose duty it is to transmit it. Filial piety discloses to us, then, in a serene light, the human wealth that God has given us and that He does not cease to give us. Through it we bind ourselves to all the generations that have preceded us. We enter into what they are. We enter into what they have made us, and we enter into ourselves.

In knowing our fathers, in understanding them, in loving them, we know our children, we become able to open the future to them, and we fashion that future. Is there anything more human, more vital, more necessary? I ask myself this.

Filial piety makes us enter into the immediate principle of our personal character and of our being itself.

It makes us worthy of the existence we have received, and it clothes that existence in its pure and authentic nobility.

The man who neglects it breaks himself away from his own roots. He is an anonymity.

Without filial piety, the individual is no longer a family being; he is no longer a social being; he is disintegrated.

Parch a shrub, uproot it, and see then whether it can flower. He who "frees" himself from filial piety is a dead man. His existence is that of a faded plant. When the plant fades, what becomes of nature? What remains of life? Civilizations and cultures that were the very brilliant contemporaries of Chinese civilizations and culture have barely bequeathed to us their pyramids, their tombs; and it is only by opening these that we can learn what they were.

Filial piety is the principle that conditions all the spiritual and moral life of mankind, from its most distant past to its uttermost future. Could not that principle, in the vast domain that is its, open the deepest and the richest vein to the enquiries of the mind and the intuitions of the heart? The Confucianist thinkers have made it the object of their calm and ceaseless endeavor. I think the depth and the richness of this vein have no limit.

In the millenary traditional China, the universal cult of filial piety, the generous efforts it has aroused in every home, have led to the formation and the general acceptance of a veritably democratic tradition of life, which has not ceased to embrace the whole country.

In the most humble village families, it was possible for a talented child to enter upon the literary studies that, through the progressive successes he could gain, opened to him successively the gates of the local town, of the provincial capital, and, finally, of the imperial capital.

The continuous development of his life of letters did not uproot him.

Filial piety being the universal foundation of education, the requirements of good manners made it, in the eyes of all, the most rigorous of duties. It followed that the honors a son might be able to attain did not draw him away from his family circle. On the contrary, everyone attributed them to his parents, who would not have been able to form in the heart of their child the virtues to which he was constantly beholden in his new pursuits if they had not been themselves already endowed with them. The whole family rose to the demands and the duties involved in the social rise of one of its members, and the low standards that make the whole existence of parvenus wretched was avoided with extreme care.

The imperial state was, then, in a position to recruit every well-born man to public service.

Humble conditions could prevent no one from aspiring to the service of the state. On the contrary, the public virtue of filial piety encouraged and induced all the *literati* to devote themselves disinterestedly to the service of the country according to the measure of their talents and their virtues. Concern for the public content postulated this largeness of view. Illustrious examples, of whom each century has left the memory, have remained glorious in the national tradition and history. They cause every Chinese to believe that in principle no position is forbidden to him and that, if Providence should so decide, all positions are open to him.

Obedience to the Natural Law and the practice of filial piety place man in a position to be inspired by the examples of the finest types of mankind.

It is for each to choose for his own masters the great personalities of his time and those of times past; to seek to read the correspondence of better men of other days; to take inspiration from it as if he could live by their side and in their school; to observe how they comported themselves toward their parents and their families, their superiors and their subordinates, their friends and their fellow citizens; how they comported themselves in private life and in public life.

The defects of the great are not less profitable to study than their good qualities, making it possible to perceive the shortcomings that it is important to avoid for fear of falling victim to them. Their good qualities, their virtues, trace the road by which every father of a family desires that his children shall travel and through which every man ceaselessly desires to bear witness to his own parents and to his ancestors and very humbly to venerate, above every creature, the Creator.

This conception is simple; it is truthful, and it is splendid. But there is one question that here presents itself: Are there very many men capable of realizing it? Has not our human nature contracted some inherent weakness that very often makes us experience great difficulty in obeying the Natural Law and that, for the vast majority, renders this happiness and this perfection apparently illusory?

Such as it is, at the age at which I have arrived and after God has given it to me to tread such varied paths, this conception of filial piety, the human virtue *par excellence*, has never ceased to impose itself in my thought and in my heart. It has remained as a constant renewal of my youth, which has prepared me for the understanding, very inadequate as it may be, of the words of Jesus: "Unless you turn and become like children, you will never enter the kingdom of heaven."[4]

But in order perfectly to understand these words of the Gospel, an enlightenment and a grace are necessary, which may complete the teaching for which the Natural Law alone is not sufficient. God, in His redeeming mercy, offers this greater revelation and this greater power to all men of goodwill.

May I pause a moment for some personal recollections?

I have told, with emotion, of the solemn translation of the bodies of my parents, on November 14, 1920, from Shanghai, our native city, to Beijing, before the Cemetery of Zhalan, to the vault I had religiously prepared for them.

Carrying out this act had given me a very deep consolation, that feeling of interior peace that accompanies every sincere attempt not to rest short of one's duty and of which the benefit is all the greater insofar as the duty itself is the more august and is the object of more sincerity and care.

It seemed to me that this was not enough. My public career had been unfolded on the international scene, and my parents, whose spirit of sacrifice had prepared me for that career, had been given a testimony to my filial piety only on the soil of my fatherland.

---

[4] Mt 18:3.

I conceived a second project, very modest. I was desirous that a work of art should express, in a European language, what is the very basis of Chinese national and family life, what the Chinese have meant by the character 孝 *xiao*, filial piety, which symbolizes the attitude and the act of a vigorous son bearing his old father on his shoulders; that is to say, bearing on himself, bearing in himself, all the life, all the goodness, the experience, and the history of the human race; bearing all that, with an indescribable respect, a profound gratitude; bearing it nobly, valiantly, to transmit it to his own children and to make of it the point of departure for all their future.

My attention was attracted by a remarkable monument set up at Bern to commemorate the conclusion of the International Telegraphic Union, the fruit of the thought and the chisel of the Bolognese master Giuseppe Romagnoli.

In 1923, for the third anniversary of the translation of my parents, I requested Signor Romagnoli to execute a sculpture that, while being inspired by a European theme, would express the Chinese conception. He took a Greek theme and achieved a masterpiece: Aeneas, at the height of the catastrophe, at the height of the burning of the city of Troy, saves his father, Anchises. By that act he saves, in the person of his father, all the ancestral treasure that he will hand on, with a humble grandeur, to his son Ascanius. As the result of a tender thought of Msgr. Costantini, to whom, in 1932, I offered this bronze, Romagnoli's work is today in a place of honor in the buildings of the Catholic University of Beijing.

If the recital of these too personal reminiscences does not weary the reader, I should like to add, to complete them, what was the divine response to the affectionate veneration I give to the authors of my days.

I had given my family vault at Zhalan the form of a chapel. My parents rest in the crypt, beneath the entrance to this modest sanctuary.

By a disposition of Providence, on the morning of my ordination to the priesthood, on the initiative of Father Paul Yu Bin, today archbishop of Nanjing, a group of my friends gathered in this chapel there to assist at the sacrifice of the Mass, which was on that day offered there for the first time, at the hands of the vicar apostolic of the city, Msgr. Montaigne, whose filial piety had caused him to represent me in that chapel before God and in the presence of the mortal remains of my parents on the very day when I was becoming a priest.

I think that Mr. Laurence Binyon was altogether right: Greece and China, East and West, are brothers and sisters. Can we any longer be ignorant of our brotherhood, live in separation, fail to understand that we are of the same family? Can we, in this family spirit and this family life, do other than provide ourselves with the completion that may be lacking in us, in order to be fully members of mankind?

If Providence permits me, I hope one day, in the light of filial piety, to approach with very profound reverence the most considerable fact in the history of mankind. I shall attempt to describe to my compatriots and my friends how the revelation and the redemption of Jesus Christ have seemed to me.

That redemption is the great meeting-place of the ways, the unique point where the filial piety of children and of men is opened upon a divine filial piety that Jesus Christ has shown us, to which He gives us the right, and which reunites the human creature with our Father Who is in Heaven.

If it is necessary to strive to imitate the great personages who give honor to humanity, so as to be oneself not too unworthy of being a man, how much—ten thousand times more—is it not necessary to give oneself wholly and entirely to following and imitating Jesus, the filial Son of the Father Who is in Heaven, in the way that He opens to us, to receive the Spirit which is His, the Spirit of the Father and of the Son?

The saints are nothing else than "les continuateurs et les imitateurs originaux, mais incomplets, de ce que fut complètement le Christ des Evangiles" (the original, if incomplete, continuators and imitators of that which was done completely by the Christ of the Gospels)[5]—Christ the only Son of the Father. We must be their pupils.

I will add: Is there in the world a single society where filial piety takes a more eminent, more effective, and more universal place than in the Christian and Catholic Church? Where paternal authority is more nobly represented, more gracious, and more strict, more merciful and more abundantly generous, than that which the supreme pastor assumes in his office of Vicar of Jesus Christ?

The moral and philosophical temper of the Chinese people, their family temper and their political temper, have given Chinese civilization a self-renewing strength comparable to that of nature, whose every season prepares a rebirth: the most severe of winters leads unfailingly to the spring.

If Chinese civilization has been able to survive all the vicissitudes of the world, that is because our people, faithful to the testament of their ancestors, have never feared ordeals; they have overcome them, having been able to learn and to understand what it is to suffer.

After the humiliations and the agonies that for a hundred years the combination of three factors has meant for them—the decadence of the last imperial dynasty,

---

[5] A phrase of Mr. Bergson to a friend of his who has had the kindness to tell me of it.

the technical progress of the Western world, and the encroachments of foreigners—the Chinese revival astonishes the world.

The millenary China finds herself at once in the midst of the modern world; and the modern world, with what it has that is less good and what it has that is better, meets, on a footing of political equality, men more ancient than Rome and Athens, who have remained erect upon the unshakable foundation of their institutions: filial piety, their treasure since a time older than the patriarch Abraham.

The century through which China has most recently come has been for her, in the international world against which she resisted, a century of political inequality. This inequality seemed normal to the whole world. What a crisis had not such an encounter necessarily to provoke in China! God helping her—for God helps those who obey Him—the Chinese people and the Chinese civilization have both passed through this dangerous crisis, this crisis very much more grave and more terrible than those at which all the empires of other times and all the most ancient civilizations of the globe have failed.

Let us come back to our own present times.


II


When God wishes to save a nation, He does not spare it sufferings. Without them peoples, like individuals, decline and lose their vigor. But He gives, in the hour of trial, "one man alone" who, faithful to his destiny, leads his own across the Red Sea and saves them.

When God, alas, wishes to chastise a nation, He sends it some proud dictator; or else, in the hour of trial, He leaves it without "men", leaving to guide it only groups of blind men and bands of children.

I have no need to mention to my English and American readers the names of the two great men who, dedicated to a high political vocation and faithful to that vocation, have saved England and America; and no more have I any need to name here the just and constant man to whom China today owes her salvation and her resurrection. Each of these three personalities, in protecting the dignity and the independence of the country whose government was entrusted to him, has made possible the common work of saving mankind.[6]

In the accomplishment of that joint task, the head of the Chinese state had to precede the others. Without him, long before war had broken out in Europe, Japan would have become mistress of Asia, and that domination would of itself have made the defeat and overthrow of the hideous totalitarian regimes impossible and illusory.

I have spoken of the Chinese crisis. All the peoples of the world are in full crisis. They endure, more dangerously than ever, the repercussions of power politics, which have not ceased to be the tradition in international relations, and of social injustices, aggravated by certain of the ruling classes, which have replaced a régime of feudal or absolutist character by an anonymous and capitalist order. In remedying the public ills, how much clearsightedness, how much courage is needed to restore social health and bring in peace!

The states are aware of the peril that is common to them, and they are dominated by the single purpose of saving themselves and preserving their identity. Their

---

[6] Given the context, it seems Lu is referring to leaders of the three nations during World War II: Winston Churchill, Franklin D. Roosevelt (or perhaps Harry S. Truman, given this additional letter was written for the English edition in 1948), and Chiang Kai-shek.—Ed.

salvation will depend upon the progress of international civilization, which, halted at a still primitive stage, reserves to each national entity the right to execute its own justice. It will depend upon the more or less near prospect of establishing a competent—that is to say, supranational—political organism, whose powers, precise and limited, may have as their object the effective protection of all the nations and the maintenance of justice between them—in other words, the application to international relations of the principles of the Natural Law, under the permanent supervision, increasingly well organized, of world opinion.

This task will be simple if the generality of statesmen everywhere conform their personal behavior to the demands of the Natural Law. Some of them hardly perceive the existence of such a law. Its prescriptions appear to them like so many shackles, whereas they are the fundamental basis of human dignity and of democracy.

The Chinese political tradition, of which Confucius collected the documents, is the fruit of more than four thousand years of existence. It is eminently realist. It extols the just mean. The just mean is not a condition of mediocrity, but a condition of equilibrium. Equilibrium is the very condition of all progress and of all ascent.

There is much wisdom in not being surprised that the circle of terrestrial happiness is never a perfect circle, that it is necessary to endure in order to grow and, in working to bring about greater justice, to bear one's own lot with moral fortitude. This wisdom contains a great wealth of joys and happiness. It forgets the sufferings of yesterday in order to rejoice in the pleasures of today, modest as they may be; avoiding bitterness, it sweetens sorrows; in time of trial, it values the least drops of joy. It is modest in its desires; this modesty permits it to receive with gratitude every grace and every gift of Heaven, every proof of neighborly sympathy.

Human equilibrium is an interior state of moral stability, the state of a clear and tranquil conscience, animated by a profound submission to the Creator, by an unwearying generosity toward one's neighbor, and by a strength that nothing can bend.

This equilibrium is the first virtue necessary in a statesman. It enables him to distinguish at a glance the artificial from the natural, the true from the false. Without this judgment, how would he be capable of governing men? This interior equilibrium enables him to comprehend the Natural Law, which is the first principle of all social life and the foundation of public happiness.

The earliest political philosophy of the Chinese people took its inspiration from these very simple aphorisms. It took as its basis the existence of the Creator of the Universe, the Most High God, *Altissimus*, 上帝, *Shang Di*. It took for its guiding principle and strove to take for its model the providential government of creation. It means, then, in principle, banishing from one's self all servility toward any man whatsoever. It requires a man, as his first duty, to obey God and to do what is in him to render to the Creator a worship that may not be too unworthy.

Starting from there, it declares, not without pride, that the sovereign authority of God is the sole source whence is derived, at an infinite distance, the authority of the head of the state. The head of the state is simply the mandatory of Heaven. His mandate, of which all our political tradition underlines the fragility, imposes on him, as his first duty, "to love Heaven",[7] in the name of which he is "the shepherd

---

[7] *Mencius*, bk. 1A:3.

of the people".[8] His obligations are heavy and unceasing. To meet them, he will choose for himself "just and religious ministers".[9] He will consider them "as the members of his own body, which will lead the ministers to regard the prince as their heart and as their bowels".[10] If the prince deviates from the truth, the ministers will know how to correct him;[11] they will refuse to tolerate the prince ever usurping "the place of Heaven".[12] Thus "the sovereign is, as it were, the heart of the people, and the people, as it were, the body of the sovereign.... When the body is wounded or suffering, the heart is so also."[13]

The religious basis of political power has been the corrective principle for all the abuses to which, one after the other, through the weakness of human nature and through its corruption, the successive dynasties that ruled the Chinese people allowed themselves to succumb. In consequence of our classical books, our political tradition never ceases to tell the emperor that "no one, in the whole world, is noble by his birth."[14] This mentality provoked many political revolutions. But it banished for all time from the Chinese heart the myth of an imperial divinity, of an emperor or a dynasty that could pretend to substitute itself for Heaven.

Applications of this principle of the Natural Law were constant. They made a discipline for many circles at the court and in the high mandarinate.

---

[8] *Shu Jing* (Book of history), pt. IV, chap. XXVII, 7.
[9] Ibid., pt. IV, chap. XVI, 10.
[10] *Mencius*, bk. 4A:2.
[11] *Analects of Confucius*, 13.15.c.
[12] *Li Ji* (Book of Rites), bk. VII, chap. XVIII.
[13] Ibid., bk. XXX, chap. XVII.
[14] Ibid., bk. XI, chap. XXXIII.

Under the influence of those governing circles, there went on from century to century a progressive endeavor to detach the religious basis from politics and morality. To that end, it was necessary to secularize the meaning of religious terms in our classical books; or rather, to "atheize" them. This was a slow task; it was pursued for more than a thousand years. Our national treasure was thereby changed and profoundly impoverished.

In depriving the Chinese people of the religious content of their ancestral heritage, political rulers blindly opened the frontiers to a foreign importation. Buddhism came into China. It was presented as a religion of a monastic form. Thanks to this monastic constitution, which responds to one of the most profound aspirations of the Chinese soul, it overran the whole of China, winning the court and the people, erecting its temples by the tens of thousands in all the towns and in all the villages, multiplying its monasteries in all the most beautiful places; giving spiritual sustenance to a number of souls, but scarcely coming to offer a spiritual framework for society, a sustenance for public life. Far from that! It encumbered the minds of its adherents with a mixture of superstitions that have kept at an altogether too low level the excellent minds of so many Chinese women and so many children. The faith that our people have combined with those superstitions is easily explained, for Buddhist literature contains very pure and very great pages, in which the human heart and the human mind escape from their miseries and insufficiencies, groping and, indeed, making mistakes, often very grave mistakes, to seek out the beauty and the goodness of God.

The field of religion is very delicate ground. Religious truth is a deliverance. On the other hand, errors, omissions, and confusions do very far-reaching damage, because religious reality is of a spiritual order and embraces the whole of life.

When I insist on the greatness and the purity of the fundamental principles of religion, of which Confucianism contains the treasure, no one will charge me with imagining or saying that any religion whatsoever overcomes the various temptations that, by a permissive disposition of God, make a moral trial of every human life. God reserves the final judgment to Himself alone. But every true religious idea is a great insight. It offers an incalculable moral assistance, which enables a man to do what is good more easily, to avoid what is evil with more care, and the better to correct his shortcomings.

Confucius vigorously declines to create a system. He presents himself as being simply a righteous man who, in the deep disorder of his times,[15] turns back to primitive institutions and asks for their restoration.

This restorer of moral and political integrity was in all things a poor pilgrim, endlessly journeying, from kingdom to kingdom, in search of a sovereign who would agree to take up the principles of the Natural Law again, so as to bring back public well-being and to give back a happy life to the people.

These efforts were vain. The enlightenment of his teaching was reserved for posterity. Today, after twenty-six centuries, it enlightens us still.

The most illustrious of his disciples, who lived two centuries after him, Mencius, set down in terms as lofty as those of Confucius himself the teachings of the Master. The century of Mencius was not very much better than

---

[15] The sixth century B.C. was in China a century of corruption, when regicides and parricides were frequent.

that of Confucius. "At present," writes Mencius, "in the whole of the empire, there is no shepherd of men who does not love to send men to their deaths." Those shepherds were, then, "totalitarians".

And he continues: "If there should be found the head of a state who does not love to send men to their deaths, the peoples of the world would lift up their heads, aspiring to enjoy his rule. They would run to him as water that of its own accord flows toward the valleys. Who could withstand such a torrent?"[16]

The cry of Mencius is universal.

The desire for a "good shepherd", the desire and the expectation of a "King of Peace"—more exactly, of a Messiah—is the theme that dominates the whole of the Hebrew writings of the Old Testament.

Confucius was the contemporary of the prophets of Israel.

The first of those, Isaiah, had pierced the future. He described the most important event in the history of men as if it had been unfolded before his own eyes: *Parvulus natus est nobis; filius datus est nobis.* It is the Nativity! *Factus est principatus super humerum eius: et vocabitur nomen eius Admirabilis, Consiliarius, Deus, Fortis, Pater futuri saeculi, Princeps Pacis* (For to us a child is born, to us a son is given; and the government will be upon his shoulder, and his name will be called 'Wonderful Counselor, Mighty God, Everlasting Father, Prince of Peace).' "[17]

Alas, the Jews, in handing down the writings of the prophets, did not succeed in respecting and preserving the meaning the prophets had expressed in them. Among them also there took place a long decline, which had for

---

[16] *Mencius*, bk. 1A:6.
[17] Is 9:6.

its object, or for its result, the alteration of the meaning of the capital and final term occurring in the prophetic writings. The Messiah of Peace, he whose kingdom would not be of this world, had become in their expectation a prince of this world—should I dare to write a "totalitarian"?—who would bring to the chosen people the enjoyment of a worldwide dictatorship. And when Jesus was presented to the great multitude, *turba multa*, and to the city of Zion itself, to which He brought redemption and life, His reception was tragic. The Lord did not conceal His august sorrow; He did not restrain His tears; for men, His countrymen, "were like sheep without a shepherd".[18]

Who shall reveal the significance of the unique words, which no other human being has ever pronounced and which no one could speak without falling beneath a burden of falsehood and pride? In the mouth of Jesus of Nazareth, they assume a sweetness that time cannot dim: "I am the good shepherd; I know my own and my own know me." "So there shall be one flock, one shepherd."[19]

Jesus, in His divine goodness, offers Himself as a sacrifice "to gather into one the children of God who are scattered abroad".[20] If we would strive anew to approach His thought, so as to try to put it into practice in the duties of public life, we could acquire at a very modest price, together with an effective knowledge of things divine, "the science of human relations".[21]

In China today, who are the disciples and the sheep of this Shepherd? In the immensity of the Yellow Continent,

---

[18] Mk 6:34.
[19] Jn 10:14 and 16.
[20] Jn 11:52.
[21] Cf. President Truman, address to Fordham University, New York, May 11, 1946.

how do these sheep and that Shepherd appear to the great mass of the population?

Chinese Christians are about 1 percent of our population. That proportion is very slight and might lead into error those who limit their observations to the data provided by this figure alone. By its message, by the devotion of its ministers, and by the zeal of its faithful, Christianity in China exercises a discreet influence in the heart of the nation of which the benefit is proclaimed before all. I give an incisive proof of it at once. According to his explicit declarations, Dr. Sun Yat-sen, founder of the republic, borrowed from Christian teaching the social and political principles of justice, of liberty, and of equilibrium that inspired his public life, all his work for the modernization of the Chinese state and the restoration of our nation. Dr. Sun Yat-sen belonged, as I also used to belong, to the London Missionary Society. He rated the Catholic Church very highly, and he sought to be admitted into her. I have not been able to learn in detail the circumstances on account of which his request was unfulfilled.

Christianity in China today is like a humble shoot from a mustard seed. Year by year it grows and develops. It will become a great tree.

Apostolic zeal and its proselytizing dynamism are essentially Christian. Their purpose is the spiritual service of others, the salvation of souls. The value of this zeal depends on the fidelity with which the apostle transmits the message of truth and of life that Jesus Christ brought to men and on the burning and yet considerate charity that animates his life. Inconsiderate zeal, which is inspired by divided motives and into which enters a greater or less part of pride and selfishness, is not a liberating zeal. Neverthe-less, since God, to further the salvation of men, is always pleased to make use of men themselves, it is necessary to take care not to demand of those who dedicate their lives to the good of their brethren that they be exempt from all the faults and all the weaknesses of which each one of us, alas, carries the burden.

The apostolic zeal of imperfect men has, by the grace of God, changed the course of the world's history. If there had been no Christianity, what would the history of Europe have been? And the history of America? Take away from Europe and America what they owe to the Bible, to the Greek and Latin culture of which the Cath-olic Church saved the wealth and ensured the survival; take away what they owe above all to the Gospels, to the New Testament, to Christian intelligence and to Christian charity, to the Holy Church, to the sense of freedom and of dignity that the Spirit of God gives,[22] and, I ask it again, what would remain of Europe and America?

Christianity is today entering more and more into China. It has already taken root there. On this soil prepared by the search for and the cult of the Natural Law, what, with the help of God, will it not be able to achieve! I cannot prevent myself from hoping and believing that China, in the course of the centuries ahead, will live, under the sign of Christianity, through a history blessed by God, simple, great, and happy.

Do the disciples of Jesus form a single flock, under a sin-gle shepherd? How do the non-Christian Chinese regard those divisions among the Christian missionaries who

---

[22] *Ubi Spiritus Dei, ibi libertas* (where the Spirit of the Lord is, there is free-dom): 2 Cor 3:17.

enter China; between the Catholic Church, which comprises two-thirds of the Chinese Christians, and the other churches and Christian denominations that send us their envoys?

The first thought that comes to them all is simply this: Christians are the disciples of Jesus, their divisions were born in foreign countries, and those among us who become Christians do not propose to become the heirs of the hostilities or the divisions that divide foreign Christians. The Catholics claim the plenitude of truth, and, as I have written elsewhere in this book, in the eyes of the non-Christian they are the most ancient of the Churches, the one that goes back to the beginnings of Christianity; they are in themselves alone the trunk and the roots; they have unity of doctrine, unity of government, unity of precept. These are, moreover, things that compel the most attentive consideration. The Protestants claim the same Gospel, variously interpreted. Catholics and Protestants alike say, We love our neighbor. And the truth of this last affirmation is everywhere evident.

It is necessary, then, to go farther back. What are the causes of the dissidences and the heresies, of the separations and divisions, that are handed down as a heritage to descendants to whom cannot be attributed the initiative and responsibility for rending a robe that they receive in the state in which their fathers left it?

I would summarize what I think in a very few words. Divisions, in the Church, are due to a local condition of weakness, more or less widespread, that went unremedied. At the source of all dissidence, one comes into sharp contact with a great many personal questions closely linked with questions of principle—and all the sequence of human passions follows after.

The patriarch Saint Benedict, of whom a pope[23]—and what a pope!—made himself the biographer, treats in his Rule of pastoral care of the "difficult and arduous task" of "directing souls and having regard to the customs of a large number". He attributes to the pastor responsibility for "the obedience of the disciples", and he writes: "The blame will weigh upon the pastor for all that, in the flocks," God, Who is "the Father of the family, shall find of least profit." That responsibility will only be met "if the pastor has exerted all his endeavors toward a restless and disobedient flock, and if their wrong acts have been the object of all his care."[24]

There are, at all times and under all circumstances, men who experience a need to break their most excellent contacts and to sever what joins them to their own roots. Saint Paul, in stating the fact, declared it to be inevitable.[25]

On the other hand, when, within the Church, certain pastors were unequal to their duties, their sheep were scattered. Many of them were without the heroism to face up to the insufficiencies and the faults for which their spiritual leaders were personally responsible, having ceased to be "the salt of the earth" and "the light of the world".[26]

Pastoral care imposes a very heavy burden. It demands an enlightened faith and a boundless charity.

In his homily on the duties of the good pastor, Pope Saint Gregory the Great, following Jesus Himself, draws a contrast between the pastor and the mercenary. The mercenary is inspired, not with a great love for the sheep of the Lord, but rather with a certain desire for lucrative or

---

[23] This refers to St. Gregory the Great.—Ed.
[24] Rule of St. Benedict, chap. II.
[25] *Oportet et haereses esse* (there must be factions among you): 1 Cor 11:19.
[26] Mt 5:13, 14.

honorific compensations, which makes him verily a mercenary. No man is exempt from that temptation. With a moral grandeur worthy of his personal sanctity and of the sovereign pontificate with which he was invested, Gregory the Great admits the danger always to accompany pastoral care. He calls it *periculum nostrum* (our danger).[27] Who has not been conscious of his own weakness before the humility of that declaration? For a very great courage is needed to be a shepherd of men, and a constant virtue is needed to exercise pastoral care without self-seeking. Is there here anyone who might cast the first stone? If in history we find from time to time weak and ailing men among pastors, those who, when insufficiencies and faults have occurred among their spiritual guides, have provoked division in the Church, have they been in that the disciples of Jesus? Have they acted in that as the benefactors of their fellows?

In the course of the centuries, very many ecclesiastical divisions have been produced in the field where the activities of churchmen and statesmen meet. Some among the former have been tempted by the desire to share political power, which belongs to the civil government. And among the latter there have been cold calculators who, to subjugate the spiritual institution founded by Christ, have set themselves to fawn upon churchmen. The difficulty of communications and the hermetical exclusiveness of political ficfs   *a fortiori* of states—led to the insane

---

[27] *Audistis, fratres carissimi, ex lectione evangelica eruditionem vestram; audistis et periculum nostrum* (Dearly beloved brethren, you have heard from the reading of the Gospel a lesson that concerns you; you have heard also what is our danger), Homily XIV, Pat. Lat., vol. 76, col. 1127. These words have been elevated by the Church to the dignity of a liturgical text (Second Sunday after Easter, Office of Matins).

presumption of partitioning the Kingdom of God, of cutting it up into local bodies, each possessing a sovereign power. The authors of this anomaly were unaware of the reality of the spiritual treasures of the Church, which they pretended to control and which they only succeeded, to the prejudice of all, in diminishing. They wounded the great spiritual family in which the men of all countries have an imprescriptible right to divine brotherhood. But the deep life of the Catholic Church, her unity, has escaped all their attempts.

These were melancholy dramas. To the Family of God they brought profound humiliations, and also glorious martyrs.

Whatever may be the origin of these schisms, when they are prolonged through one or several generations, it needs the help of time to bring back peace. Thanks be to God, we are again traveling uphill; the air is becoming purer and lighter; we are drawing near to the "high pastures".[28]

It is necessary to define the terms in which, in the political society of today, the problem of Christian unity is posed. This problem affects the spiritual life of men in every country of the world, the moral progress of all populations, and the public well-being of all states. It presents a particular relevance in the countries whose Christian religious history is subsequent to the division of Christendom and that did not know the quarrels from which these dissidences were born.

The unprecedented development of the means of communication has created completely new social and political conditions, a worldwide society that could not have existed hitherto. It is composed of all nations, peoples, and

---

[28] Cf. Ezek 34:14.

races. This society, as I have observed already, is deprived of all established law and of all machinery of government. It is in consequence in complete anarchy.

We are at the exceedingly dangerous stage at which brute force has, on a worldwide scale, free power to call a halt to all progress and to let loose every catastrophe.

It is important, then, as quickly as possible to provide this new political condition with supranational legislation, based on the principles of the Natural Law. To establish that legislation, to prescribe it, and to impose its application, constituted bodies are necessary that will have the powers that worldwide public order requires.

Recourse to the Natural Law is the one and only way open to the world if we are not to see the globe transformed into the worst of jungles. The Natural Law has for its basis faith in God. That basis is unique and unshakable.

Toward the end of his speech at Buenos Aires on December 1, 1936, President Roosevelt, describing the "old hatreds" and the "new fanaticisms" that have thrown European society into confusion, insisted on the necessity of "faith in God" to protect "faith in freedom", to protect "the democratic form of constitutional representative government" and "the security of the individual".

He observed:

> Before man knew how to record thoughts or events, the human race has been distinguished from other forms of life by the existence, the fact, of religion. Periodic attempts to deny God have always come and will always come to naught.
>
> In the constitution and in the practice of our Nations is the right of freedom of religion. But this ideal, these words, presuppose a belief and a trust in God.

This faith is that of the Western world.

After what we have said of the political institutions of China, my readers will understand that this same "faith in God" is the first and unshakable foundation of the civilization and of the life of the Eastern world. Parallel attempts to deny it, which, there also, have been periodically made, have likewise utterly failed.

If the political partitioning of the world and the primitive stage of international civilization have been major causes or occasions of the division of Christendom, will not the irresistible progress of that civilization and the organization of supranational political life have as their result the disappearance little by little, as of their own accord, of a great number of the factors that have broken and that frustrate the unity of Christendom? Those obstacles to unity that but yesterday still seemed insurmountable!

This problem is too great not to be solved victoriously.

When the Most High gives us that victory, it will be a triumph for the human race. No man, on the other hand, will be able to attribute the merit and the honor to himself, for we are all of us poor sinners. The glory of it will revert to God.

It is for Him to reunite us, not within the walls of a Tower of Babel, but in the bright light of the sun, on "the high pastures", under the incomparable crosier of the Good Shepherd.

### III

I have told of the predominating influence of Christianity on the person and on the work of the founder of the Chinese republic. Through him, and through those of his collaborators and successors who share the same faith, that influence has been extended to the very evolution of the Chinese state and the Chinese people.

That evolution and that revolution are being achieved without detaching the Eastern world from its Confucianist foundations, which are the foundations of the Natural Law; on the contrary, those foundations are found to be singularly strengthened by Christian principles, and we are therefore enabled to build an extremely stable edifice, whose strength will be enough to endure through as many ages as our history has already passed through, and more.

So far as the present spread of Christianity and of Catholicism in China is concerned, I should like to draw attention to the very great significance of the religious events that, in the course of these recent months, have taken place in the Catholic Church in China: the establishment of the hierarchy, the entry of a Chinese member of that hierarchy into the Sacred College, and the appointment of Chinese bishops to the archiepiscopal sees of Beijing and Nanjing.

Every initial effort is necessarily a particular act.

Missionary labors, duly approved by the Holy See, have not escaped that character, which sets in relief, on the one hand, the generosity of their pioneers and, on the other hand, the clearsightedness and disinterestedness of those who today are carrying that work beyond the particular applications suitable to its beginnings but obstructive to its development.

For every initial effort is necessarily confined to a limited field; to a single region, and often to a single social circle.

The great Jesuits of the seventeenth century had aimed at the head; they had entered into direct relations with the Imperial Court. My countrymen have not yet been able to understand how it was that their methods, so eminently charitable and so judicious, were able to give place, especially in the nineteenth century, to an evangelization too easily confined to the lower strata of the population and to the illiterate. Even more than at the present time, the Protestant churches were addressing themselves to the intelligentsia of the country, setting up in China more than twenty universities, and, despite their condition of dissidence with regard to the Universal Church, attracting much sympathy to Christianity. That condition of dissidence is unhappily a great weakness, which especially manifests itself when certain of our separated brethren seem to take offence at the evangelizing light of the papacy and perhaps even sometimes at its existence.[29]

The hour has come for all to lift up their heads. It is not an attitude of pride. It is an attitude of faith and of hope, of humble bravery, of living charity.

He who abjures his personal particularism—in other words, his selfishness—brings himself inevitably nearer to the universality, to the "catholicism", which is the mark of the goodness of God.

In making the Sacred College more and more international, at a time when the development of the means of communication makes this possible, since it transforms the terrestrial globe into one single city—in preparing for the new developments in the same direction that Providence may indicate, the Holy Father has undertaken a work that two or three centuries hence will have extended the fold of Jesus Christ to those millions of righteous men, "from every nation", "from all tribes and peoples", and

---

[29] We have noticed recently (May 1946) the attitude of various Protestant churches and associations in the United States, reproaching President Truman for sending a personal representative to the Holy See. Protests of that kind take on in the eyes of a Confucianist a character that is not very becoming, which underlines instead of concealing the abnormal condition in which members of the Christian family hold themselves at a distance from the Father of the family and take offence at his deeds of universal generosity.

"tongues"[30] of whom the theologians declare that they belong to "the soul of the Church".

The pope who, half a century from now, will preside over the second millenary of the birth of the Savior will be the august witness of that evangelization of which the nineteenth century and the beginning of the twentieth could have no inkling, the certain signs of which the divine mercy today permits us to discern.

In preparation for this future, we must open our eyes and our hearts, abjure all narrowness and all illusions of a provincial mind, make ourselves aware of our weakness and of our strength, and not close our minds to the thought that the number of Chinese Christians, Catholics, and Protestants still does not exceed a very slight percentage of the population.

*Pusillus grex!* "Fear not, little flock, for it is your Father's good pleasure to give you the kingdom";[31] that kingdom is on this earth, but, assuredly, it is not of this earth.

The present head of the Chinese state, he who, after Sun Yat-sen, had to save the nation and the people from twenty floods at the same time, is, even as was Dr. Sun himself, a disciple of Jesus.[32] By a providential coincidence, of which the astonishing significance has not been sufficiently pointed out, these two statesmen have experienced, at a distance of forty years, similar ordeals, of a character at once political, moral, and religious.

On October 1, 1896, the revolutionary Sun Yat-sen, being in London, fell into a trap prepared for him by the imperial legation of China. Imprisoned, illegally, in

---

[30] Rev 7:9.
[31] Lk 12:32.
[32] This refers to Chiang Kai-shek, who was an observant Methodist.—Ed.

the legation building at 49 Portland Place, he was detained there for twelve days, in the course of which plans were made for his secret transference to China, where death awaited him. He saw himself and knew himself to be lost. He derived from "incessant prayer, night and day during the first six or seven days of his captivity", the spiritual mastery that enabled him to win over his jailer and to gain his help in freeing himself. The iron-barred garret that served as his prison has been made into a commemorative chamber. It is a shrine of the Chinese nation.

Forty years later, on December 12, 1936, Generalissimo Chiang Kai-Shek, being at Xi'an fu in the course of his duties as commander-in-chief, fell into a trap prepared for him by the "reds". All his bodyguard having been killed, he was for thirteen days in imminent danger, from one moment to the next, of being executed. He persuaded them to give him a Bible, and he derived from meditation on the Passion of Jesus Christ the spiritual mastery that enabled him to win over the whole band of his jailers; they set him free on the afternoon of Christmas Day. There and then, in imitation of Jesus, the commander-in-chief pardoned those who had made the plot.

These identical ordeals through which God led in turn the founder of the republic and the head of the state reveal to us the religious foundation of all that each of them gave in the service of the fatherland and of the state.

Filled with respect for every sincere conviction, President Chiang Kai-Shek conceals from no one what his spiritual life gives him. Quite recently again, in his message for Christmas 1945, he called upon the Christians of China, "Protestants and Catholics", to pray, to dedicate themselves, and to sacrifice themselves for the fatherland. He added: "Our nation as a whole needs the faith, the high standards, and the spirit of sacrifice of Jesus," "the Savior of mankind".

*Pusillus grex!* (Little flock!)

On March 22, 1946, His Eminence Cardinal Tian,[33] the first among Chinese prelates to become a member of the senate of the Church and to share with her head the responsibilities of the worldwide government of Christendom, did me the great honor of coming to see me at the Abbey of Saint Andrew. The Holy Father had graciously given him his approval of this visit.

The cardinal invited me to return to China, in order to take a personal part on the soil of my fatherland in the development of the Church and in that also of my country. This invitation, this great honor, and the apostolic warmth and the affectionate insistence that marked it, gave me a renewal of ardor and of joy. It was with great delight that at once I disposed myself to respond to this appeal. I prepared for my return.

Some weeks later, on May 16, His Holiness Pope Pius XII, in an act of august benevolence, deigned to confer the abbatial dignity upon me, of the title of Saint Peter of Ghent, an illustrious monastery founded in 630 by the Apostle of Belgium, Saint Amand, whose monastic and evangelizing career has thus given me a program and an example. The Abbey of Saint Peter of Ghent lived through nearly twelve centuries, up to the French Revolution.

In the course of his visit to Saint Andrew's, Cardinal Tian was solemnly received in the Saint Andrew Chapter House. He drew the attention of his hearers to the sovereign importance, for the evolution of China and the growth of the Church and of Christianity in my country, of the ten years now beginning. The hour has come for the *pusillus grex* to advance, humbly and bravely, into

---

[33] Refers to Thomas Cardinal Tian Gengxin 田耕莘, named archbishop of Beijing and cardinal in 1946.—Ed.

the front line. Renouncing all personal considerations and comforts, the Catholics of China will give themselves in total sacrifice for this unique task: to bring to the civilization of the Far East the message of Jesus Christ, and, with it, "the Kingdom of God".

I should like here to invoke the words of an Anglican.

In his *Parochial and Plain Sermons*,[34] Newman devoted a magnificent page to the divine plan of wisdom and strength in virtue of which a few men only, and not a great multitude, were "chosen before of God" to bear effective witness to the Resurrection of Jesus and to present that fact to the faith of the whole world. "It is, indeed," he observes, "a *general* characteristic of the course of His providence to make the few the channels of His blessings to the many." These few men Jesus "formed into Himself, that they might show forth His praise" and that they might be made capable of transmitting to others the same witness, the same truth, and the same life. "St. Peter's disciple, Ignatius," was "a feeble old man" when, before the Roman emperor, he bore triumphant witness to Christ. "Ignatius was one against many, as St. Peter had been before him." "But he handed on the Truth, in his day."

It is with consolation that, to address myself here to my friends in Great Britain and America and to describe to them the program that God has given us, I take again these words of Newman and encourage myself in the thought that the divine strength which was that of Saint Peter and Saint Ignatius is offered to us all and that old age and weakness present no hindrance to it.

Sons of Saint Benedict, come from Rome and from Monte Cassino, gave the Christian faith to Britain, and

---

[34] Vol. I, no. XXII. Anglican sermon preached on April 24, 1831.

they founded there the Catholic Archbishopric of Canterbury, in the period when Saint Amand founded at Ghent the Abbey of Saint Peter.

In memory of these origins, a distinguished group of English cathedrals, of Oxford and Cambridge Colleges and of parish churches of the same confession, one and all founded in other times by the Benedictines, have wished to renew contact with the Mother-Abbey of Monte Cassino, destroyed and desolated by the war. Joined in this notably by the Anglican Church Assembly's Commission for Aid to European Churches, of which the bishop of Chichester is chairman, they have decided to take a share in restoring scholarly life to the cloisters where Saint Benedict wrote and published his immortal *Regula Monachorum* (Rule of the monks).

The delicate thought that inspires this generosity, and the gratitude it expresses, touches us all the more since it comes from dissident Christians, since the divided condition of Christendom grieves us deeply.

Seeing how lively remains the memory of those first Benedictines, envoys of Christ and of Peter to the Anglo-Saxons, how could I not beseech God that He may call from Great Britain and America "a few men only", "chosen before of Him", to bring to the Far East the monastic work of evangelization that was accomplished in England in the seventh century and that, a hundred and fifty years later, holy English monks continued in Central Europe.

The ways of God are inscrutable. At the time when Newman spoke the words I have quoted, no one foresaw that fourteen years afterward he was to find again the fullness of the Christian message that sons of Saint Benedict had brought to his country.

The ways of God are mysterious. And that is why, in our faith and in the charity that God gives us, we have a filial confidence in His Providence. That confidence fills us with an audacious and an invincible hope.

In the invitation that I permit myself here to extend, so natural in a Christian, a monk, and a priest on whom an Englishman conferred baptism, there is, as everyone will see, very much more than a most profound desire to further the Christian life in my own country.

The good that we are doing and to which we invite our neighbors is not only a sowing of happiness and of life for those who receive it; it is, in the first place, for those who give it. When a father and a mother give life to a child and help one another in educating it, they both grow much more in human value and in dignity than their child grows; it must wait for the age of maturity to become in its turn a father or a mother, to give itself to those whom it will have begotten and whom it will educate, and to attain the dignity and the stature that its own birth meant to its parents.

All is glorious for those who understand that greatness is in the gift of self, whatever may be the form the giving takes.

It is glorious for a European to hand on to a civilization very much more ancient than his own the torch of the divine Christian life that Europe received before Asia.

It is glorious for a Chinese to accept that same torch from his juniors.

And when the light is spread through all the world, if the wind of human passions may here and there quench some few of its flames, the Christians of other places will hasten to light them again. In this mutual gift of light, there are no longer either juniors or seniors, either first-comers or last-comers, because for God there is no distinction of persons, and because the title of "Son of Heaven", handed down through thousands of years to the successive heads of the twenty-four dynasties that occupied the throne of Beijing, has been transformed with a new grandeur and a new meaning to become, as I wrote at the conclusion of my *Souvenirs et Pensées,* the divine and "democratic" title of every man coming into this world who accepts the Spirit of Jesus and becomes in truth a "child of God".

THE FEAST OF THE HOLY APOSTLES PETER AND PAUL.
June 29, 1946

*Cum permissu Superiorum*

# INDEX